How I Turn Ordinary Complaints into Thousands of Dollars

How I Turn Ordinary Complaints into Thousands of Dollars:

THE DIARY OF A TOUGH CUSTOMER

RALPH CHARELL

STEIN AND DAY/*Publishers*/New York

First published in 1973
Copyright © 1973 by Ralph Charell
Library of Congress Catalog No. 73-81323
Designed by David Miller
Printed in the United States of America
Stein and Day/*Publishers*/Scarborough House, Briarcliff Manor, New York 10510
ISBN 0-8128-1616-1

FIFTH PRINTING, 1974

When I was about ten, I traded a kid my age who lived up the block a quite serviceable pair of roller skates and two dollars for an old but working Stromberg-Carlson radio-phonograph. This was the first deal I ever made, and for a few hours I was elated. Then the kid and his mother rang our doorbell—and everybody turned on me. With some difficulty, I was able to piece together the message that, by virtue of my superior intelligence, I had victimized that kid. The transaction was reversed, the skates and the two dollars were handed over and I skulked off to fetch the radio-phonograph.

For the next twenty some years I made nothing but bad deals. Invariably, I felt called upon to completely protect others from me and "my superior intelligence" and they wound up being insured against every contingency, including acts of God. Time after time I wondered why I had again come up holding the short end of the stick—until I remembered that kid and the Stromberg-Carlson.

Because I no longer make bad deals, I'd like to dedicate this book to Messrs. Stromberg and Carlson, wherever they may be.

Contents

Introduction

There's a story about a man who always read the Travel and Resorts Section of the Sunday *New York Times* but never took a vacation. One week, he saw an ad for a ten-day cruise to eight Caribbean islands for only $34.00. All one needed to do, according to the ad, was bring the money to the river end of Wall Street at 9:30 A.M. the following Saturday. Incredulous, our man followed the instructions. But when he arrived at the specified place, he found it deserted.

Suddenly, out of nowhere, a burly fellow appeared and staggered our man with a blow from behind. The next thing he knew he was chained to an oar, as were a number of other people who'd read the ad. An overseer with a whip kept the rowers in tempo. Every three hours there was a short break for gruel.

The cruise ship did, indeed, call at eight Caribbean

islands during the next ten days. While the better-accommodated, freer-spending passengers above went ashore, our man and his comrades below, still chained, were permitted to sleep. After ten days, the ship arrived at its berth off Wall Street. The burly fellow who had clobbered the thirty-four-dollar passengers appeared below and ordered the rowers, now unlocked from their respective oars, off the ship. Our man approached him.

"Excuse me," he said. "I've never been on a cruise before. How much do you tip the whipper?"

While this story is apocryphal, countless variations of it are being enacted daily by surly clerks, cost-cutting manufacturers and indifferent professionals. The incidence of these everyday atrocities is rising exponentially. The resultant toll in destroyed nerve endings, abraded stomach linings, and crushed spirits is incalculable.

Whereas in the past, he who paid the piper called the tune, nowadays he has forfeited that choice and is barely tolerated within listening distance. The time-honored basis of supply and demand, which balanced buyers and sellers for centuries, has become distorted, perhaps destroyed. Barely remembered and regarded as quaint is the time when the customer was always right. Customers and clients are treated as mewling cretins or unwelcome intrusions on the private gossip or rich fantasy life of the typical company employee.

Standards of all kinds are disappearing—the two-by-four has become the one and five-eighths by three and five-eighths; the dollar is something of a misnomer; and God has been declared dead.

The world has become a global *city*, a place of short weight, squelched self-esteem and numberless daily social muggings. We are nurturing a race of cringing Lilliputians, trained from infancy to accept and expect the hindmost. We are becoming a new breed of transient and suspicious strangers unable to cope with ordinary situations we deem too big for our own efforts to alter or affect.

Too many have been paying too much for too little too long. Surely, the whipper's gratuities are overdue for curtailment.

More and more often, we are forced to deal with unaccountable employees of large conglomerates, or faceless bureaucrats whose telephones are busy, out of order, or worse, left unattended while they filch an extra coffee break or otherwise extend their on-the-job semiretirement. Shoddy, overpriced goods and poor services are a commonplace.

What can be done to correct these imbalances? All too often, the amount of time and effort involved may seem prohibitive, or we may fear that our credit rating is subject to computer annihilation if we justifiably withhold payment. If we are to be relieved of being continually tossed up in blankets, thrown down interpersonal air shafts, stuffed into social drain-spouts, and put on hold buttons that end only in disconnect signals, we must come up with a new approach. New methods of coping with myriad affronts, intransigent rudenesses, deceits, incompetencies, obfuscations, procrastinations and other unwelcome business practices must be developed quickly if we are to survive.

In the chapters which follow, I have attempted to find new solutions (like one-way bridge tolls) to old problems. Some worked immediately; others never, and these were discarded. As in judo, I often used the weight and size and momentum of the other side against it. I discovered that if a large corporation has numerous employees who lack both concern and jurisdiction, the proper executive, correctly motivated, will dispense other people's money (the stockholders') with astonishing speed. Once I became aware of the seemingly boundless incompetence of others, I traded on it by anticipating it and reversing the ordinary procedure—by complaining first, then sending the order and payment. There are many pressure points and, with practice, they are easily grasped.

The results of this experimentation have been extremely rewarding and lots of fun. Handling my own complaints has become a source of pleasure to me—a relaxing break from demanding professional tasks.

Although I do not consciously seek such controversies, they have a way of overtaking some of my most innocent pursuits. Once I get involved there is no turning back, and so far my record is perfect. Skill, persistence, and the will to win are important, but nothing counts as heavily as knowing your cause is just.

My methods, as outlined in this book, can be used by anyone. However, I should point out that effective complaining is intended as a means of self-defense, not as another kind of attack, and never as a rip-off. One should defend oneself with honor, but never so vigorously as to become the aggressor. With the knowledge that one could, if necessary, prostrate a given adversary, one may well decide not to do so, with dignity.

The examples that follow might lead one to assume that I have spent disproportionate time and effort in these pursuits. Perhaps I have in some instances, if success is measured by money alone. But the time I use is always down time and represents, in the aggregate, much less than many people spend on hobbies. The adversaries I challenged always had far greater resources than I. Usually they were large corporations which were clearly, often admittedly, in the wrong, yet resistant to the usual appeals. Although there may have been times when I received more than I deserved (not including the value of my time), that was never my original intention, and it occurred only after the other side had steadfastly refused a lesser settlement. Rationalization? Maybe. But I think I've been fairly reasonable, and I know I feel a lot better now that I've learned from my own experience that the "givens," in everyday transactions, are not immutable. They can be challenged—and changed.

A Washing Machine

After giving us months of excellent service, our washing machine began to leak. The problem seemed to be caused by a leaky piece of rubber tubing or a faulty connection. My wife called Korvettes, where we'd bought the machine, and learned that its warranty had expired. She was advised to call the Franchised Service Corporation, which would come and repair it at a reasonable price.

After breaking the first appointment, two men from Franchised arrived at our home and announced themselves as "Air conditioning!" They thought they had been sent to remove an air conditioner from our apartment (as Franchised also repairs air conditioners), and they had brought the tools with them to do so.

My wife pointed out that it was a washing machine, not an air conditioner, which needed repair, and asked whether they had brought a replacement for the piece of rubber tubing she had minutely described over the telephone. They had not. They removed the faulty piece of tubing from the machine, demanded and received $10.50 plus tax for the "house call," and promised to return and actually repair the machine in the not-too-distant future.

That night, when my wife summarized the above events for me, it seemed clear that we were being charged for one house call too many. The next morning, I called the man in charge at Franchised. I explained that if his men had known what they were doing, they would have brought the ten-cent piece of rubber tubing in the first place; therefore we should pay only the additional cost of the tubing and not for the second house call. Otherwise, I told him, Franchised could return our money and we would go elsewhere.

The Franchised man, in turn, offered me a choice: either I would pay for two house calls plus the price of the part, or they would keep our money and we could go elsewhere.

"Very well," said I. "I will call the store which recommended you and, hopefully, you will be hearing from them soon."

I was shuttled and shuffled from employee to employee, endlessly telling and retelling my dreary tale while my days turned to nights, my mind to jelly. Those who might have helped were busy or vacationing or in meetings. Those I was able to reach didn't understand or lacked jurisdiction. It seemed to me that the Vice President in Charge of Customer Relations was the man who could set things right, but he was never in when I phoned and never returned any of my calls.

A little research revealed that Korvettes is part of a conglomerate owned by Spartans Industries, whose chief executive officer was named Charles Bassine. Many businesses are parts of larger companies, and I have often found it easier to deal with the parent. I usually ask the executive office switchboard operator of the company being difficult whether there is a parent company. One call to the parent will almost always yield the name of the company president—after all, this is public information. If the name is not immediately forthcoming, it is available at any local brokerage office in Moody's or Standard and Poor's corporate records, or in most public libraries.

Armed with the chief executive's name, I again called the Vice President in Charge of Customer Relations and was told that he was not at his desk, which came as no surprise.

"In that case," I told his secretary, "perhaps you could give him a message."

"Is it short? I don't take dictation."

"It's not long, and I think Mr. Green* will consider it rather important, so I'll speak slowly while you copy it down."

"What is it?"

*All names in this book which are those of colors are fictitious. All the other names of people and companies are actual.

"My name is Jennings," said I. "I represent the Charells. . . ."

I explained that the Charells were having some difficulty with Franchised and gave her the address and the model number of the faulty washing machine, as well as the name of the man Charell had spoken with at Franchised and his telephone number.

"The Charells have called the store many times, including a number of calls to Mr. Green, to no avail. As I was only recently remarking to my old friend and classmate, Charlie Bassine, 'Isn't it a shame that people like the Charells have to call upon me to handle a matter like this when there undoubtedly must be somebody at the store who has that responsibility.' Charlie informed me that Mr. Green was the man to contact. I would suggest that he get a brand-new machine over to the Charells right away so that Charlie won't have to get into this matter personally."

"He just came in, Mr. Jennings. Would you like to speak with him?"

"That won't be necessary. Just give him the message, please. Also, tell him I assume he can have the Charells' money returned from Franchised, as they have done nothing to earn it."

"I'm sure he can, Mr. Jennings. May he get back to you later in the day?"

"As a matter of fact, I'm on my way to the airport right now. I'll be down in Houston on another matter for a couple of weeks but I'll be calling my client in a couple of days to find out what Mr. Green has done."

The next morning, before I left for the office, two men delivered a brand-new machine inside a sealed container, and took away the defective machine. About a week later, an envelope arrived from Franchised containing the piece of rubber tubing they'd taken and their check, reimbursing us in full for the "house call."

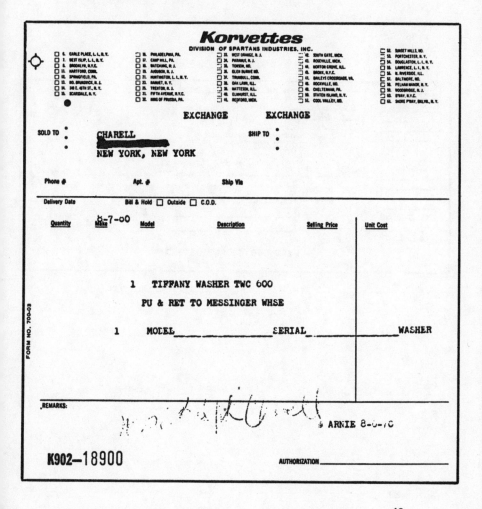

19

FRANCHISED SERVICE CORP.
1178 EAST 180TH STREET
BRONX, N.Y. 10460

1-797
260

Refund of service
call - part
undesirable

ROYAL NATIONAL BANK OF NEW YORK
826 EAST 149TH STREET
BRONX, N.Y.

NO. 3772

Pay _____ ᵗᵉˢᵘ · ⟋ ⟋ DOLS ⟋ 3 CTS _____ Dollars

to the order of _Mrs Chavell_

Check No.	Date	$
3772	7/31/70	11 13

FRANCHISED SERVICE CORP.

B _William A. Fowlerglan_

AUTH. SIG.

⑆0260⑈0797⑆ 642 0527 ⑈⑈

Slipshod

After trying on a pair of black shoes at Saks Fifth
Avenue, I decided to take them, as well as the same
style in brown. When I got them home, I found that
the lining in the back of one of the brown shoes was
crunched up. The next day, I called the store and
explained the problem. I suggested that instead of
making two trips, a store messenger could pick up
the defective shoes and deliver another pair at the
same time. The salesperson checked and told me that
the store did not have that model and size in stock,
and that the order would take about three weeks.
I offered to keep the damaged shoes until the
exchange could be made, but was told that the store
preferred to pick them up at once and deliver the
new pair later.

The brown shoes were picked up, and about three
days later a delivery was made. The same shoe was
crunched up in the same place, and as I had been

told that the store was out of that color in my size, I realized that they must have redelivered the same defective pair of shoes.

It seemed pointless to spend so much time on a pair of shoes. I called the shoe department at Saks and told the salesman to have the shoes picked up and credited to my account; I would buy my shoes elsewhere. The shoe man told me that only the Customer Service Department could arrange what I wanted. When I asked him to transfer the call, he told me that was impossible. I therefore asked him if he would be kind enough to take my name and address and forward the facts to Customer Service.

"I told you," said the man, "it's out of my hands."

"I bill between a hundred and a hundred and fifty dollars an hour for my preemptive time," I said—an exaggeration, but one which can instantly restructure most situations. "I've already spent so much time on this rather small matter that there is no way I can break even. If you cannot take my name and address and pass it along to wherever it has to go, I will have to tell Mr. Bedford* you refused to accommodate me."

"All right," relented the man, "I'll take care of it."

A week later, the shoes were still in my foyer. I called the store to find out whether the salesman had arranged to credit my account and have the shoes picked up. The Customer Service Department told me that their forms were made out in quadruplicate

*The store manager.

but that United Parcel Service got all four copies, so there was no way of checking. Could someone check with United Parcel? No, that would be very difficult, but Customer Service would be happy to put the papers through "again" and could assure me that United Parcel would be picking up the shoes soon.

"But that's exactly the point," I said. "I'm trying to find out whether this is the first or second time the papers are being processed."

The next moment, I was connected with a man who wondered whether he could help me and said he reported directly to Mr. Bedford. On hearing my story, he apologized and told me that he would send a special messenger, not United Parcel, to immediately pick up the brown shoes and credit them to my account.

"You know," I told this gentleman, "even as we speak, I'm wearing the black shoes, and I hope you won't mind my saying this, but they seem rather shoddy at the price I paid." I had already pointed out my usual billing rate and my dim chances of breaking even on this transaction. I added that I had been dealing with the store for a generation without any problem. "The last time I bought shoes at the store they were also about forty-five dollars but they were much better made. I hope you won't take this personally, but these shoes, frankly, are junk."

"In that case, sir, I will be happy to send a messenger for the black shoes as well and credit both pairs of shoes to your account."

"That *sounds* reasonable," I replied, "but when I took the time to go shopping at Saks, I did that because I needed shoes. I've also spent over a week trying to straighten this out. Now, if you take both pairs of shoes away from me, I won't have the shoes I need and I'll have to begin all over again."

"What do you want?"*

"Well," said I, "under the circumstances, in view of all the time I've had to put into this matter, I'd like you to send the messenger to pick up the brown shoes, and I'd like to keep the black shoes—but not pay for them."

"Done!" he said.

"Just a moment. I don't think that's fair to the store. After all, even though the shoes are admittedly junk they must have cost the store *something*."

"Sir, I insist!" said the man.

"Why?"

"Because we don't want to lose you as a customer." I accepted that reasoning and his follow-through was faultless.

*Whenever I hear this question I know I'm on the right track.

Saks Fifth Avenue

611 FIFTH AVENUE. NEW YORK, N. Y. 10022 • PLAZA 3-4000

ACCOUNT NUMBER
19-113-794

MR RALPH CHARELL

H1   5

NEW YORK N Y

REGULAR ACCOUNT
CYCLE 2

PLEASE SHOW ANY ADDRESS CHANGE

NUMBER AND STREET

CITY   STATE   ZIP CODE

$_____
AMOUNT ENCLOSED

PLEASE RETURN THIS PORTION WITH YOUR PAYMENT

REGULAR ACCOUNT TERMS	REFERENCE MO. DAY NO.	STORE	CHARGES	CREDITS	PAYMENTS
REGULAR ACCOUNT TERMS: FULL PAYMENT OF NEW BALANCE IS DUE UPON RECEIPT OF STATEMENT.					
	1103 143	01	89.88		
OPTION ACCOUNT TERMS: YOU MAY PAY THE ENTIRE NEW BALANCE WITHIN 25 DAYS OF THE CLOSING DATE PRINTED ON THIS STATEMENT TO AVOID ADDITIONAL FINANCE CHARGES.	1104 177	01	44.94		
	1111 064	01		44.94	
OR	1116 042	01		44.94	
IF YOU CHOOSE TO MAKE A PARTIAL PAYMENT (NOT LESS THAN THE MINIMUM PAYMENT DUE AS SHOWN ABOVE), A FINANCE CHARGE WILL BE ADDED, COMPUTED ON THE PREVIOUS BALANCE AFTER DEDUCTING PAYMENTS AND CREDITS AS PER THE SCHEDULE BELOW. IF A FINANCE CHARGE IS SHOWN IT WAS COMPUTED IN THIS SAME MANNER.	1127 005	99		44.94	

CLOSING DATE MONTH DAY YEAR	PREVIOUS BALANCE	PAYMENTS & CREDITS	BALANCE SUBJECT TO FINANCE CHARGE	OPTION ACCOUNT FINANCE CHARGE	CHARGES	▼ NEW BALANCE ▼
1205 72	0 00	134 82			134 82	0 00

PAYMENTS, CREDITS, OR PURCHASES WHICH ARE NOT SHOWN ON THIS BILL WILL APPEAR ON YOUR NEXT MONTH'S STATEMENT.

INQUIRY REGARDING ANY ITEM SHOULD BE ACCOMPANIED BY THE SALES CHECK OR CREDIT SLIP.

SAKS FIFTH AVENUE, NEW YORK SEE REVERSE SIDE FOR OUR STORE LOCATIONS

OPTION ACCOUNT - SCHEDULE OF FINANCE CHARGES		
BALANCE SUBJECT TO FINANCE CHARGE	MONTHLY PERIODIC RATE	ANNUAL PERCENTAGE RATE
TO $	%	%
OVER $	%	%

25

People in Glass Houses

One Friday I walked into Steuben Glass and picked out a glass koala bear which I wanted sent to the West Coast as a gift. When I told the salesman that the gift had to arrive the following Thursday, he assured me this would be no problem. For an additional eight dollars it would be sent air express and insured. I told the man that if there was any doubt about delivery, I could get the gift to its destination myself in one day. He replied that this procedure was routine and that if I sent it, it would not have the Steuben Glass insurance coverage. I wrote a check for two hundred eighty-eight dollars, handed the man a card to be enclosed, and left.

The following Monday, just to make sure, I called the salesman at Steuben Glass and asked if the koala bear had gone out. The man assured me that he had taken care of it personally and had even checked the piece for scratches. The gift would certainly arrive by Thursday, as promised.

On the Friday after the gift was to have been delivered, I spoke with its intended recipient. I inferred from the fact that I was not being thanked that something had gone wrong.

I called Steuben Glass and asked my salesman for the waybill number and the name of the carrier, so I could check the delay myself. After a pause, he came back to the telephone to tell me that he was terribly sorry but the gift had gone out by registered mail on Wednesday.

"Registered mail!" I exclaimed. "That's the United States Post Office. I have no control over it and no way of finding out what went wrong. And how could it have gone out Wednesday? You told me on Monday you'd taken care of it. This is very unpleasant. I'd like to speak with a corporate executive."

"This is Mr. White," said the next voice in my ear. "We're terribly sorry, Mr. Charell. It's entirely our fault. I cannot get the gift delivered yesterday, but what else can I do for you?

"Before we discuss what you can do," I replied, "I'd like to review what you've already done." I went over the story for him.

"We're terribly sorry, Mr. Charell," said Mr. White. "You are certainly entitled to the difference between the cost of air express and registered mail."

"The difference in postage! I didn't go to Macy's! I went to Steuben Glass!"

"Under the circumstances, we'd be willing to send another koala bear and simply have the party refuse the second package that arrives so that it will be returned to us. If we send the gift today by air express, it will probably arrive tomorrow."

"I'm afraid that won't do, Mr. White," I said. "In the first place, I wanted the gift to arrive yesterday and as you correctly pointed out, you cannot cause that to happen. The date of delivery was an essential of the transaction, as stated at the time. Second, there is a message in the first package which won't be in the second one. But above all, the occasion for the gift is now passé. The entire purchase price is somewhere in the drainage as far as I'm concerned, and I am sustaining a further collateral loss because of the way this matter has been handled. I can't imagine how anybody could have thought this gift could be sent on Wednesday by the U.S. Post Office and arrive across the country the following day. If this is the way the company handled this item, I am wondering how many other customers are being similarly treated. I don't want to make any accusations, but this transaction seems to have many of the elements of fraud. Perhaps I ought to take this up with Mr. Buechner."*

"We'd be willing to refund your money."

"I'm not sure I understand you. Do you mean you want me to get back a gift I gave somebody, return it to the store and get my money back?"

"Keep it," he sneered.

*Thomas Buechner is the president of Steuben Glass.

"I don't think that's fair to the store."

"Well, what do you *want,* sir!"

"Well, despite the fact that the entire transaction is a total loss for me, I don't think the store should sustain a total loss. Under the circumstances, I think a rebate of some sort would be in order."

"That's penny-*ante,* sir!" said the same gentleman who had earlier offered me the difference in postage.

"Perhaps you're right," said I. "In that case, I accept your offer."

"The paperwork will take some time but I'll get it started at once," said Mr. White.*

A few days later I received a letter of apology and a check for $288. I wrote to Mr. White thanking him for the understanding manner with which this matter had been handled and regretting the fact that the company had taken a loss. I also assured him I would attempt to make up the loss by purchasing future gifts from Steuben. Mr. White responded, as a postscript to "the unfortunate affair of the koala," that the gift had arrived shortly after we'd spoken and the receipt had been returned.

*This man was dispensing money that actually belonged to the Corning Glass stockholders, just as the man at Saks Fifth Avenue was dispensing Gimbels' stockholders' funds. Had these gentlemen been co-owners of a candy store, it is extremely doubtful that either of them would have parted with a quarter. This is another demonstration of the fact that corporate executives are managers and not owners; although they may be more difficult to reach than owners, in general, once you have their attention and properly motivate them, they are willing to dispense other people's money with surprising alacrity.

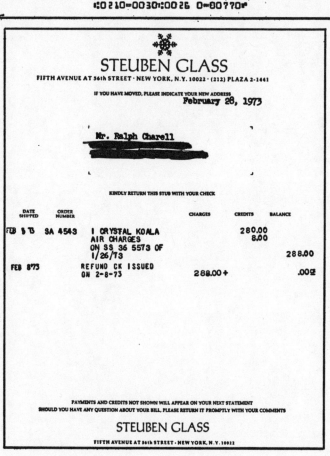

STEUBEN GLASS, A Division of Corning Glass Works   R   2577

SPECIAL FUND ACCOUNT

NOT VALID AFTER 30 DAYS

New York February 8   19 73   1-30/210

PAY TO THE ORDER OF   Mr. Ralph Charell $ 288.00

TWO HUNDRED 208 AND 00 CTS   DOLLARS

COUNTERSIGNATURE REQUIRED OVER $300.00

MANUFACTURERS HANOVER TRUST COMPANY
741 Fifth Avenue, New York N. Y. 10022

1973
2/8   refund   288.00

TOTAL OF INVOICES
LESS DISCOUNT
LESS
TOTAL DEDUCTIONS
AMOUNT OF CHECK

⑈0210⑈0030⑈0026 0⑈80770⑈

STEUBEN GLASS

FIFTH AVENUE AT 56th STREET · NEW YORK, N.Y. 10022 · (212) PLAZA 2-1441

IF YOU HAVE MOVED, PLEASE INDICATE YOUR NEW ADDRESS

February 28, 1973

Mr. Ralph Charell

KINDLY RETURN THIS STUB WITH YOUR CHECK

DATE SHIPPED	ORDER NUMBER		CHARGES	CREDITS	BALANCE
FEB 8 73	SA 4543	1 CRYSTAL KOALA		280.00	
		AIR CHARGES		8.00	
		ON SS 36 5573 OF			
		1/26/73			288.00
FEB 8 73		REFUND CK ISSUED			
		ON 2-8-73	288.00+		.00½

PAYMENTS AND CREDITS NOT SHOWN WILL APPEAR ON YOUR NEXT STATEMENT
SHOULD YOU HAVE ANY QUESTION ABOUT YOUR BILL, PLEASE RETURN IT PROMPTLY WITH YOUR COMMENTS

STEUBEN GLASS

FIFTH AVENUE AT 56th STREET · NEW YORK, N.Y. 10022

31

Conversations with Ma Bell

Several years ago, we moved from one apartment to another in the same building and had our telephones reinstalled. From the first day, they failed to work properly. When we dialed five digits of a telephone number, the telephone would often disconnect itself. Strangers would dial a number which was not ours and wake us up in the wee hours. Friends would attempt to call us and hear a telephone ringing while our phone remained silent and we were thought to be out. While we talked with somebody on the phone a number of different conversations would cross and we were suddenly plugged into the lives of people all over the city.

Our reasonable request for a new phone number was refused. We had to get an additional telephone line and a number of additional jacks in order to have any reliable telephonic link with the outside world. Because our second line had the same three-digit prefix as the original, we realized that many of the phone company's explanations about problems in the central office were nonsense.

Over the course of three years of telephone plague, we were able to piece together a sufficiently recognizable picture so that we (not the telephone company) were able to suggest a solution. The telephone was finally repaired.

I called the business office of the phone company and cited the years of interrupted sleep, missed social and business calls, countless wrong numbers, and other disturbances we had suffered because of the malfunctioning phone. I offered to waive all of our claims if they would simply rebate us a small percentage of what we had paid them for their "services" over the period in question. I asked for two hundred dollars, which was about twenty per cent of what I had paid. The company checked their records, and offered me thirty-seven cents.

I replied that I was rejecting that settlement but was curious as to how the thirty-seven-cent offer had been computed. It seems that a pro rata rebate was in order only if the subscriber had no service for a consecutive forty-eight-hour period.

I pointed out that, under that ruling, if a subscriber had no service every other day he would be entitled to nothing, which was patently preposterous. Nevertheless, I was told, thirty-seven cents was their best offer.

During 1971, I spoke with more than 30 people

at the telephone company in an attempt to settle this matter. When a caller asks to speak with Mr. William Ellinghaus, the President of the New York Telephone Company, he is connected with one of Ellinghaus's assistants. The caller explains the situation to the assistant who, if he is competent, is quickly promoted into another job and never heard of again. The choice seemed to be between speaking with a competent person once or incompetent people often. The procedure could hardly be better designed to eliminate all but the most persistent. I dealt with the business, commercial, and legal departments, all to no avail.

Finally, I decided to call the Public Service Commission. In every regulated industry—public utilities, securities, insurance, banking, etc.—there is a regulatory state or federal agency which can be of great help to the consumer. In the case of the phone company, the regulatory agency is the PSC. After getting some information from the PSC, I wrote the following letter:

March 11, 1971

Mr. P. Q. Plaid
New York Telephone Company
140 West Street
New York, New York

Dear Mr. Plaid:

In accordance with your request in our telephone

conversation yesterday, the following are some of the relevant details:

The telephone number involved in this matter is 212-348-4785. The top line of my current bill is in the amount of $12.11; this may or may not include the additional telephone number 212-348-3712, which I had installed about 15 months ago in order to insure some means of telephone communication with the outside world.

The 4785 number was originally installed at 1147 Park Avenue in the name of Julianne Andrews, which was my wife's name prior to our marriage. This number was carried over to the 57 East 88th St. address, Apartment 3D, in December, 1965. This same number was carried over when we moved into another apartment, 2C, in the same building (57 East 88th St., the current address) in April, 1968.

We have had a multiplicity of troubles with this line from its original installation up to a few months ago. An army of repairmen have failed to solve the problems. There have, in fact, been resulting damages; I have personally called scores of telephone company employees, most of whose names and the relevant details, etc. I have in a file, and I have spent a great deal of my own time trying to cope with this problem.

At this point, as we discussed on the telephone, I would like to make a last attempt to settle this claim at this level.

Owing to the lack of candor and repeated failures to return the majority of my calls, I asked the PSC to furnish me with the line card on this number. I am told that there are seven pages of troubles since 1968 alone. This information, decoded, will be in my hands in a couple of days.

After you have had a chance to review the facts, I would appreciate hearing from you.

Sincerely,
Ralph Charell

Mr. Plaid offered me a settlement of about $46 on the condition that I give up my second telephone line. That is, if I gave up the one telephone line with which I had had no difficulty for years and kept the one that plagued us, they would give me forty-six dollars. After explaining that this would not do, I asked the PSC to get from the telephone company a list of all of the problems with our phone their records showed over the period and forward the list to me. The telephone company claimed that its records did not go back to April 1968 (when the troubles began) but did furnish the partial list set forth on the following page:

COMMISSIONERS
JOSEPH C. SWIDLER
CHAIRMAN
EDWARD P. LARKIN
JOHN T. RYAN
WILLIAM F. WALSH
WILLIAM K. JONES

IN REPLY REFER TO Y 4412

STATE OF NEW YORK

PUBLIC SERVICE COMMISSION
199 CHURCH STREET
NEW YORK, N. Y. 10007

March 19, 1971

Mr. Ralph Charell
New York, New York

Dear Mr. Charell:

        In accordance with your request we have obtained
the following information from the New York Telephone Company
regarding the service problems which you have had:

DATE	TROUBLE FOUND	TROUBLE FOUND CAUSE & WORK DONE	DATE & TIME OK
5/15/69	Dial out of order Busy trunking		
5/16	Checked ok Dial out of order	Saturday 11:05 pm.	5/17/69 10:15
5/17	Call-back sub, didn't know what it was about. Please call later	ok circuit	
10/21/69	Crossed with 872-4785	Before 3 today ok to sub.	10/21 11:00
10/30	No dial tone extension out		
10/30 10:25	Circuit ok-repairman was out to premises. exten.io.: out	Sub says ok now	10/30 2:15
11/24	Keeps hanging up-cut off		
11/24	Gets cut off, sub wants wires and instrument inspected today-1/5.	Cleared off normal?	11/24 2:30
11/28/69	Irate, calling everyday. customer reaches operator, can't call thru, reaches wrong number.		

38

11/28/69	Cover inside 11/29 busy talking 2:20 circuit ok 2:35	(Central office)	11/29
12/11	Checked ok	can't call out at times, suggest change of equipment as precaution on reported trouble	12/19 6:20
12/3		Central office cover issued #966	
12/19/69	reaches wrong # wants promised visit	12-20 no trouble found	12/19 8:00
2/7/70	can't call or receive calls subs. irate	ok to sub.	2/7 8:01 pm.
2/14/70	no dial tone		5:40 pm.
2/15/70 12:25	hung up on 48 verified in	reran to out- going trunk TT # 20	2-15 2:45
2/16 6:10	Circuit ok 10:40 A	ok to sub. Wants 2 phones replaced CVW portable white 13' mounting cord Tues. 9-12	
2/14	Dead		
2/15	Replace phones no dial tone	replaced CV white- CV w-white 13' mounting card	2/17 10:45 A
2/17	Inter-Presidential complaint. Poor service. Called Mrs. Charell and apologized for inconvenience		
2/24	out of order c. ok can't meet incoming	ok to sub.	2/17 2/25 10:35

-2-

3/1070	PSC 2594 22 months terrible service, repair out many times-no satis- faction-wants rebate	3/11 Central office cover # 611, can't call and reaches wrong numbers. 3/12 returned Central office cover-no trouble found
3/12	contacted sub-said service has been good since 2/17. Complaint was with amount of rebate. This was worked out with Mr. Haas of Bus. Office. 1 month rebate was given.	
9/21	wants new CV-white 13' mtg. cord wants replaced	9/23 replaced CV white 9/23 1:30 P
11/5	open; wrong conductor, class A	348-2929 on 11/5 pair-hung up 7:30 P double conn. relay check ok to sub.
12/28/70	out of order, open Main distributing frame,bell rings, can't meet; crossed wires. Checked ok, inspect out as precaution 9:15	no access,sub 12/29 returns after 9:45 New Years. Cleared short circuit at 42 A 12/30 12:00
12/30	Inter-Pres. Complaint sub. claims repeated trouble for yrs., had Central Office cover made on 12/30-# 1954 Central office cover-reran R 2 　　　　　#1954 N.T.F. on return of cover	
12/30 5 Pm.	no wires at bridging heads	
1/5/71	referred for special attention	made all channel test outgoing N.T.F.
1/6/71	Mr. Charell wants to talk to someone in authority	
1/7/71	Mr. Charell wants change of tel. and rebate for 5 years of service problems. Will not accept number change until case is settled.	
1/27	Central office equipment change ok.	
1/28	service ok past week	

Thank you for the opportunity to be of service

Very truly yours,

Charles Kraft

CHARLES KRAFT
Senior Telephone Engineer

CAD:jg

I then requested a hearing with the PSC:

March 26, 1971

Mr. Charles Kraft
Public Service Commission
199 Church Street
New York, New York 10007

Dear Mr. Kraft:

Thank you very much for your letter of March 19.
Referring to Y 4412, I would appreciate your scheduling a hearing as soon as conveniently possible for the following reasons:

I have had years of malfunction with my telephone, 212 348-4785, which go back to the day this line was installed. Over the years of difficulties with this line, the telephone company has steadfastly refused to give me a different telephone number. (In this connection, I subsequently installed an additional telephone line in order to have a telephonic connection with the outside world).

41

There have been numerous misstatements of fact made by the telephone company. At this point, after spending many valuable hours attempting to communicate with the New York Telephone Company in an effort to settle this matter, it is clear that this avenue is unavailing. Therefore, I would much appreciate your setting down a date for a hearing on this matter at your early convenience. I would also appreciate your notifying me who will be present to represent the telephone company.

Sincerely,
Ralph Charell

E.M. Boylan and W.G. Swinney appeared on behalf of the telephone company.

E. M. Boylan
Manager

New York Telephone Company
201 East 69th Street. New York. N.Y. 10021
Area Code 212 ~~385-4500   Ext. 7030~~
TR9-9992

The two telephone company employees, the PSC man, and I sat about a table as I outlined the complaint. After some give and take, it became clear that the entire procedure was intended merely to mollify a customer but to produce no real relief. Therefore, in order to get their attention and cooperation, I decided to raise the stakes.

"I think we can wrap this up rather quickly," I said. "Before we had this hearing I was willing to settle for two hundred dollars. Now it's five hundred, and if I have to bring an action against the company it will be for fifty thousand dollars. I think even without a jury, any reasonable judge would be willing to grant at least fifteen per cent of that. And if that doesn't do it, I think I can have the company nationalized within three years."

There was a hush in the room. The others silently looked sideways at one another. It reminded me of one of those typical scenes from a B-movie in which the scientist and his assistant see another sign of craziness strewn about and the scientist, before a fade, tells the assistant: "We're dealing with a warped mind." But this was precisely the desired effect. The hearing examiner cleared his throat: "How would you go about doing that, Mr. Charell?"

I then pointed out a few possibilities which it would not be fair to repeat and concluded by saying:

"One of my closest friends manages major talent. Among his clients are some of America's highest-paid comics. Part of his job is to book these people in nightclubs, concerts, television, etc. How would it be if he had some of these well-known comics say during some of their appearances, strictly as a joke, of course, that people who feel dissatisfied with the telephone company should take a pencil and push it through some of the holes in the computer card when they return it with their payment. In this way, the telephone company would be forced to deal with them individually and not simply lump them together impersonally in a machine. Now you know better than I that if only one per cent of the subscribers did this, you would be up to here with clerical work that you would have great difficulty handling until some genius decided to use a magnetic strip at the top or bottom of the bill. In which case, how difficult would it be for the same or other comics to say, simply as a joke, of course, that those who still feel aggrieved should simply tear off the magnetic strip? You would have no way of coping with this difficulty and the government would probably have to step in to help you.

"By the way, if you're looking for a rationalization which will allow you to reimburse me without having to include all of your other subscribers, why not find out what you did to repair my telephone and work it backwards? In this way, you should be able to figure out how poor the services must have been all these years."

The two telephone representatives looked at each other for a moment and then turned to me.

"If you will give us your assurance that you will do nothing, absolutely nothing, for two days, I think we can settle this matter to your satisfaction, Mr. Charell," said one of the representatives.

"I've waited several years. I don't see how two more days can make much difference."

There was no doubt in my mind when I left that room that the telephone company would figure out a way to offer me a little more than two hundred dollars.

Two days later, I was asked if $208.39 would be acceptable—which it was, it was.

New York Telephone *Thank You!*

See the front pages of
your telephone directory
for information on:
• Charges for calls
• Your Business Office
  phone number
• Payment locations

RALPH CHARELL

NEW YORK NY

AREA
CODE
483
MAY 4 71

		STATE TAX AND ANY OTH. TAX	FEDERAL TAX INCL	AMT
MONTHLY CHARGE FOR SERVICE • Message units included	75	63	104	1211
ADDITIONAL MESSAGE UNITS •	60 #	20	33	383
CALLS AND TELEGRAMS • See Statement				
OTHER CHARGES OR CREDITS				
DIRECTORY REPRESENTATION • Explanation enclosed				
BALANCE FROM LAST BILL • Please disregard this amount if paid				9586
	KXXX R		TOTAL	11180

\#   2 MSG UNITS DEDUCTED FOR OPER CREDITS

NEW YORK TELEPHONE COMPANY

Date June 16, 1971

Ralph Charell

New York, NY

CHARGES: Balance Due on Bill Dated:_____

CREDITS: By Payment $_____ Date_____

Credit Balance Stamps *Check Herewith	96	59

* Please Deposit Check Promptly
No Receipt is Required

STATE OF NEW YORK
PUBLIC SERVICE COMMISSION
COMMUNICATIONS DIVISION
COMPLAINT SECTION

199 CHURCH ST.   REFER TO Y#
NEW YORK, N. Y.   10007

THE PUBLIC SERVICE COMMISSION HAS
BEEN INFORMED BY THE NEW YORK TELEPHONE COMPANY
THAT THE BILLING OR SERVICE DIFFICULTY RECENTLY
REPORTED TO THE COMMISSION HAS BEEN CORRECTED.

IF FURTHER DIFFICULTIES ARE
ENCOUNTERED, PLEASE CONTACT US AT 488-5330 AND
REFER TO THE Y NUMBER AT THE TOP OF THIS CARD.

Renting Not Just a Car But a Company

Some time ago, I took a business trip to the West Coast. After dinner, I called the Hertz agency at my hotel to arrange a rental, but the office had closed for the night. I called the toll-free number in Oklahoma City that was indicated on my credit card and told the agent who answered that I was staying at the Beverly Hills Hotel, that I wanted to rent a car for seven days beginning at 9:30 the following morning, and that I had the special gold card which entitled me to a Thunderbird at the price of a Ford. When I was informed that the gold card was valid only at the airport, I settled for a Ford LTD, to be picked up at the hotel at 9:30 AM the following day. I was told that my reservation was confirmed.

The next morning, after an enjoyable breakfast at the hotel, I went to the Hertz counter to pick up my car. The charming Hertz woman had never heard of me. I explained that I had made the reservation through the toll-free number, but she assured me she had nothing in my name. In order to save time, I asked whether, regardless of the misplaced reservation, I could rent a Ford LTD at once. There were no cars available. I then gave her the three-digit identification number of the agent I had spoken with the previous night.

Further checking revealed that the agent had made my reservation at the airport, not at the hotel. When I asked how soon the car could be brought from the airport to the hotel, I was told that it was impossible. What other cars, then, were immediately available? The woman told me that there was only one rentable car in the garage, a Javelin.

"Surely, you must have something bigger than that."

She admitted that there was a Cadillac in the garage, but it had been promised for the following day.

"That's perfect," I said. "I'll take the Cadillac now and get it back here tomorrow morning. Then I can exchange it for the Ford LTD which is now at the airport, and pay the weekly rate for the Ford. What time will you be needing the Cadillac tomorrow?"

Oh no, said the woman, that would not be possible, and besides, the Cadillac rented for twenty dollars a day plus twenty cents a mile.

I returned to my room, called the New York office

of Hertz, and was soon speaking with Mr. Sky Blue. After explaining the situation to him and throwing in a choice *non sequitur* (often a time-saving device*) to the effect that if I did not quickly arrive at my destination, the picture would have to go into what the unions laughingly call golden time and would cost about two thousand dollars per hour.

The vice president was most understanding and told me that as far as he was concerned I could have the use of the Cadillac for the entire term of the contract at the price of the Ford. I thanked him and said that would not be necessary. I would simply use the Cadillac for a day and exchange it for the Ford, at the price of the Ford. He agreed to call the Hertz office at the Beverly Hills Hotel so that I could be on my way.

When I returned to the Hertz counter, the woman was already engaged in conversation with Mr. Sky Blue. She seemed to be in complete agreement with whatever he was saying. Finally, she hung up the telephone and said:

"You're in luck, Mr. Charell. Soupy Sales just returned a Ford LTD to the hotel. Exactly what you wanted."

"Madam," I replied with a smile, "Soupy Sales is

---

*In the typical complaint call, the other party is busy and wants to get to the bottom line as soon as possible. Your opening remarks shouldn't elicit much conversation. If you are in the right and can easily be helped, the person will want to help you.

a performer, not a mechanic. I want a car that's been fully serviced—like that Cadillac."

The woman, good-natured sport that she was, threw up her hands and began to make out the papers.

The Wrecker's Ball

The most profitable matter I've handled on my own behalf involved the demolition of a building in which my wife, daughter, and I lived, at 57 East 88th Street in New York. The landlord had purchased our building and five surrounding buildings with the intention of demolishing all six and putting up a huge co-op apartment complex.

This plan first came to our attention one quiet summer evening (July 9, 1969) when we were served with a paper which said in part that "unless you remove from the said premises on the thirty-first day of August 1969 . . . the landlord will commence summary proceedings under the statute to remove you from said premises . . ."

As our lease did not expire until the following spring, we were not unduly alarmed. However, virtually all the other one hundred twenty-three tenants in the buildings were statutory (their leases had expired and new leases were never offered), and this paper produced well-calculated panic among them. Good apartments like these—in solid, old buildings, well-located, at relatively modest rentals—were simply no longer available in New York.

The tenants began to organize their resistance. Those in our building met in one of the apartments and formed a legal committee, which I was asked to join. The committee (three lawyers, a doctor and myself) recommended hiring a lawyer who specialized in landlord-tenant cases and asked each tenant to contribute an initial sum of one hundred dollars toward the legal fees.

The committee narrowed the choice of lawyers to two. One was said to be a veritable tiger for tenants' rights; the other was said to be extremely competent and, I heard later, was related to one of the members of the committee. I was not personally familiar with either lawyer but voted for the tiger, who lost three to two.

On July 28, 1969, the chosen lawyer presented an agreement which called on the tenants to pay him $3,000 on or before August 11, 1969. If the tenants were in possession of their respective apartments one year later, an additional $3,000 was to be paid. In addition, the lawyer would receive twenty-five per cent of the monies which any tenant received for surrendering possession of his apartment. The tenants were to further agree not to negotiate directly with the landlord; but in the event they did, the attorney would nevertheless be entitled to the amounts set forth above. In return for these considerations, the lawyer agreed to undertake certain "class actions."

The tenant who had proposed the tiger and I told the other members of the committee that we would not sign such an agreement, could not recommend such an agreement to the other tenants, and would seek our own remedies individually. After some conversation, we resigned from the committee. In a subsequent meeting with the tenants, the attorney the committee endorsed was approved, although the terms of his retainer were modified somewhat in favor of the tenants.

As time wore on, a number of apartments became vacant. Some wealthy tenants wished to avoid unpleasantness and left rather quickly. Some older women left because they were frightened. Other tenants settled for relatively small sums of money and moved out. One by one, the four smaller buildings in the parcel were vacated and demolished.

The New York Rent Control Law requires an "official" relocation period, usually lasting one to four months, in which the landlord must make a formal written offer of a new apartment to each tenant. The apartment must be "suitable," as defined by the Rent Office. After a number of informal offers had been made and withdrawn, my family was formally offered an apartment in Brooklyn. We had a prescribed period in which to reply:

June 1, 1971

Mrs. Esther L. Moscow
HDA Dept. of Rent and Housing Maintenance
Relocation Section
110 Church Street
New York, New York 10007

Dear Mrs. Moscow:

This letter includes a number of reasons for our rejecting Apt. 6-J at 441 Ocean Avenue.

First, however, we should like to repeat that the so-called previous apartment offerings at 46 E. 96th St. and 1230 Park Avenue were never formal offers (please see attached). Additionally, the apartment offered at 215 W. 88th St. was withdrawn (see attached letter). We would therefore appreciate your instructing Mr. Simon to delist the first two apartments as having been previously offered.

With respect to Apt. 6-J at 441 Ocean Avenue, there are a number of reasons why this apartment is not suitable or appropriate for us. The following, for the sake of brevity, includes, without being limited, a number of these reasons.

We were surprised to arrive more than a half hour late to our appointment with the superintendent as we had no idea that the subway ride from our apartment would take more than one hour and twenty minutes (with good connections). The return trip, with good connections on three express trains, took one hour and twelve minutes. Our daughter, Leslie, is a rather small, frail child. Leslie has been attending private schools since nursery school. No school she has attended has been farther away from where we live than twelve minutes by bus. Leslie is currently registered at The Trinity School in Manhattan. In order for her to arrive at the prescribed time in the morning she would have to be awakened at approximately 6:00 AM and then be subjected to a long train ride. This long train ride would have to be repeated twice each school day, adding more than two hours of travel time to the day. The chronic deprivation of sleep and rest added to a school day lengthened by more than two hours of travel time would be an intolerable burden on the child's health and well-being.

It is interesting to note that one or more tenants, similarly situated, offered an apartment in Brooklyn, found such apartment voluntarily withdrawn by virtue of the same kind of private school situation. Not to do so in this case would be discriminatory.

Additionally, my husband is approximately fifteen minutes from his office by bus, the distance being approximately a mile and a half. My husband has been under the care of doctors for a permanent back injury for more than twenty years. Being forced to stand for over an hour each way in rush-hour subway conditions would be an insupportable burden on his health.

Additionally, the school at which I teach is located within five or six minutes' walking distance. To add more than two hours of travel time by subway each day would be burdensome. It should be pointed out that the subway trips we made in looking at the offered apartment took us from one express stop to another express stop. Neither my school, my husband's office or our daughter's school is located at an express stop, thus requiring even more time and changing of trains than indicated. It should also be pointed out that none of us is forced to travel by subway; currently, we are able to get to our destinations on foot, by bus, bicycle and taxi. These safer and more desirable means of transportation would be impractical if we were forced to live in the offered apartment.

The offered apartment contains only one bathroom. Our current apartment has one and a half baths. Thus, in the offered apartment, we would be caused undue discomfort, particularly during those times when my husband, for medical reasons, takes long, hot baths and this is done on a daily basis and as prescribed by a doctor.

The offered apartment has no doorman, whereas our apartment has a doorman. This fact, coupled with a large, unprotected courtyard with several places not within the sight lines of anybody entering the building and no security system whatever, in a high crime area, would, at best, produce continuing anxiety for me and my daughter. It should be pointed out that this neighborhood has been plagued by day and night muggings and burglaries.

A number of apartments in the building are rented at considerably below $100 per month. The apartment we have been offered is in no reasonable way comparable to ours, except in price, and that price would also be subject to change, presumably, under the new rent law.

In all fairness, Mrs. Moscow, even without mentioning the small size of the rooms and their condition, it is difficult to understand how any reasonable person could find the offered apartment suitable and appropriate for us.

Sincerely,
Julianne Charell

Enclosures
cc: Messrs. William Simon, M. Bruce Solomon (no
enclosures)

With astonishing speed, the Housing and Development Administration reviewed the matter and made their determination by return mail:

HOUSING AND DEVELOPMENT ADMINISTRATION
ALBERT A. WALSH, *Administrator*

Department of Rent and Housing Maintenance
BENJAMIN ALTMAN, *Deputy Administrator/Commissioner*

Office of Rent Control
110 CHURCH STREET, NEW YORK, N. Y. 10007

M. BRUCE SOLOMON, *Deputy Commissioner*
DANIEL W. JOY, *General Counsel*

Date: June 2, 1971

Mrs. Julianne Charrel

New York, New York

Re: Docket No. 2E 8359-8454

Dear Mrs. Charrel:

We have received your rejection of apartment number 6-J
at 441 Ocean Avenue, Brooklyn
offered for relocation by your landlord.

This Administration has reviewed the reasons given for your refusal
and has determined that the apartment is suitable and in accordance
with our regulations, however, we have asked the relocator to make
informal offers of apartments in your neighborhood.

Therefore, you have ten days from the date of this letter to accept
this offer. Rejection on your part or failure to respond will mean
that your landlord is not required to make additional formal offers
to comply with our relocation regulations and will only have to pay
you a stipend in accordance with the self-relocated schedule after
you vacate your present accommodations. If you wish to discuss our
determination, you may call Mrs. Esther Moscow at 566- 4458.

Very truly yours,

ESTHER L. MOSCOW
Relocation Director

ELM:vc

cc: Mr. M. Simon

2S

While this matter was being processed, there were many attempts to save housing like ours. A neighborhood association filed a suit to block this specific project, bills were introduced into the City Council, and magazine and newspaper articles and editorials appeared opposing this sort of huge, mid-block structure.

THE NEW YORK TIMES, SATURDAY, JUNE 27, 1970

Save the Side Streets

No one really seems to know how the area from 86th to 96th Street between Fifth and Park Avenues got to be zoned solidly "R10," but that is how it turned out in the revised zoning law of 1961. To translate numbers into buildings, this means that the very large apartment houses permitted on the avenues are also permitted on the side streets in these ten blocks. Below 86th, the side streets are zoned "R8," which preserves "valleys" of smaller structures and lower densities between the avenue blockbusters.

Translating buildings into neighborhoods, this mixed zoning of "R8" type also means Manhattan's characteristic balance of small and large, high and low, and the "side street style" that is its notable virtue and ambience. The pattern has created an area of special residential amenities that include sun, light, scale, architectural and environmental variety and simple humanity. Exactly those things that make the area desirable would be wiped out by the destruction of the side streets for high-density apartments. This is one case in which it is not possible to have one's cake and eat it.

Translating neighborhoods into people, the side streets contain sound, older housing where it is possible to live for less than the going new-building luxury rate of $125 a room. Community groups have asked the City Planning Commission to save the side streets from 86th to 96th by rezoning them to match the prevailing lower densities to the south.

It is difficult to accept the developers' argument that it is proper and desirable to wipe out good middle income housing that cannot be duplicated and to build instead a stereotyped upper-income ghetto. It is more difficult to accept their claim that unless new luxury apartments are located in this narrow range of the upper East Side where executives prefer to live, corporations will not come to New York, eroding its national headquarters position and its tax base. The further erosion of the middle class is a dubious and dangerous tradeoff.

The basic zoning dilemma that New York faces goes much farther and deeper than these ten blocks. It is citywide and almost insoluble. Virtually every attempt to provide higher density housing in order to meet the housing shortage is in direct conflict with the preservation of the dwindling quality of the city's life and the narrowing margin of its supporting services. New York's interlocking problems make it resemble nothing so much as a house of cards. In the case of this curiously mutant uptown zoning, the 1961 designation is obviously destructive. To change it now undoubtedly entails serious legal and financial complications. But the issue is environment, not economics, and the latter, alone, will never keep a city alive or worth living in.

A number of minor unpleasantnesses developed. For example, our ancient stove, which we had inherited from another apartment in the same building, was getting progressively worse. Whenever the oven was used, choking fumes would pour out. The building superintendent was willing to exchange our stove for one from a vacant apartment, but was prevented from doing so by one of the landlords, a Mr. Slate.

I told Mr. Slate that the fumes were harmful to our health and that we could make the exchange at no cost whatever to him. He said that my presence at one of the preliminary hearings before the Housing and Development Administration indicated my unfriendliness and that "un-friends" don't deserve any consideration. I replied that becoming aware of my rights was a privilege afforded me under our form of government and should not be interpreted as unfriendliness, but that not attending to this dangerous and harmful stove was a violation of the building code.

When further conversation failed to change his attitude, I arranged for a city inspector to examine the stove. The following day, after filling out the necessary form, I called the real estate office and spoke with Mr. Slate. I explained that three violations on the stove were already being processed and that I had on my desk a form requesting an "abatement of rent for an abatement of services" which was filled out and ready to be mailed to the Department of Rent and Housing Maintenance. I pointed out that when a copy of this form came to the attention of the other landlords, he might look rather foolish, but that he could avoid all this with one telephone call to the superintendent of our building. He agreed to make the call, and an acceptable stove was substituted the following day.

When our apartment was due to be repainted, the landlord refused to do so and then contested our request for an abatement of rent for failure to paint. All of the lobby furniture disappeared, was said to be stolen, but after some complaining, mysteriously reappeared.

For days on end, refrigerators and toilets were stored in the lobby of our building.

Against this background, the landlords and I were negotiating. What I had to sell was time. There were a number of ways to delay our eviction and all delays, after a certain point, could be extremely costly to the landlords. They were dealing with what I estimated was a ten-million-dollar project, including acquisition costs, loss of rents, building and interest costs. The earlier they could build, the lower would be their costs and the sooner would their profits begin to flow. But they couldn't build until all of the tenants had moved out.

The time factor was a very interesting variable from my point of view. If I delayed the landlords until the day before we were to be evicted, it would not be worth their while to pay us anything—so I couldn't overplay this aspect. My objective was never to jeopardize their project or to penalize them by remaining in the building alone after all of the other tenants had vacated, but only to get a fair settlement.

It was a delicate situation and one in which the landlords held most of the cards in the deck. At all times, I would have been happy to accept a reasonable buy-out, but we could not agree on what was reasonable. Furthermore, if the landlords paid us a relatively large sum while several other tenants remained, they feared that the other tenants would demand an equal amount. This made it extremely difficult for us to come to terms while other tenants were in the building.

During the course of our negotiations, I tried to make the point that my family was faced with at least an additional two hundred dollars per month for a comparable apartment and that an extra twenty-four hundred dollars per year after taxes for the single item of rent was not a pleasant prospect. We reached a verbal agreement that they would pay the differential in rent for five years on an apartment which they found for us, which was acceptable, and which actually rented for something under two hundred dollars per month additional. In addition, we would receive the sum of one thousand dollars, which I estimated would cover our moving expenses.

Almost as soon as Mr. Slate and I reached this agreement, I received a telephone call from a different landlord who told me that Mr. Slate did not have the authority to make that agreement. This is one of the standard ploys in bad-faith dealings. I replied that I was reserving the right to insist that future offers be made in writing and properly authorized.

In the meantime, I continued to build my case. I hired The Title Guarantee Company to provide me with a record of building-code violations on the building in Brooklyn in which the "suitable" apartment for us had been offered. I also kept monthly statistics of the seven major crimes as reported by the Federal Bureau of Investigation for the precinct in which the Brooklyn apartment was located as compared with the precinct in which we then lived. I was under no illusions about our relative strengths and realized that I was going against one of the Goliaths of the real-estate industry in the city. I had also been warned many times, not always politely, that unless we reached an agreement, we would be put out on the sidewalk with nothing more than the legal stipend (a few hundred dollars).

As our building became progressively less

occupied, my wife and I discussed the possible dangers to our daughter and ourselves. I was thus under some additional pressure to reach an agreement with the other side and did, in fact, reach a second verbal agreement which was substantially less than the original verbal agreement. The landlords reneged on the second agreement as well. I was then offered a third settlement, substantially less than the second. This offer was accompanied by a take-it-or-leave-it ultimatum. I did not like this offer or the manner in which it had been made but, in discussing it with my wife that evening, it was clear to me that the question of our physical security was beginning to trouble her. We agreed that I would attempt to improve the offer as much as I could and settle with the other side, which I did. However, the contract I received offered considerably less than had been agreed to, and therefore constituted a reneging on the third agreement.

I didn't sign. Instead, I told my wife that I had never really liked the third agreement and now that it had been whittled down further, our correct response was to take a firm position. This meant we had to be prepared to outstay all of the other tenants. I considered the problem of our security and concluded that it was extremely doubtful that the landlords, responsible and reputable business people, would cause us physical injury. Nevertheless, I promised my wife and daughter that if they requested it, I would hire an armed guard to be posted outside our door, who would escort us to and from the building. We consulted the yellow pages and were enchanted by a number of illustrative ads which promised uniformed armed guards with trained dogs. After I rejected the third offer, I got a telephone call from Mr. Slate. I made it clear that we were not interested in deal number three, or in either of the other two deals, and that we had no further interest in negotiating at this time.

"At this point, we're at war, Ralph," he informed me.

I tried to make it clear that I wanted and fully intended to make a deal at a later time, and had no intention of blocking the project or penalizing the landlords with excessive delays. I reminded him that it was he and his colleagues who had broken three agreements, and suggested that they would probably deal more legitimately with me if I waited until all of the other tenants had signed agreements.

We were being inexorably pushed toward the day when, if we failed to reach an agreement, the marshal would remove our furniture from the premises. Relocation procedures were exhausted. The fifth building in the parcel was vacated and demolished. Certificates of Eviction were issued on each remaining tenant in our building. This meant that after a four-month waiting period, the landlords could attempt to obtain a court order to evict us. Under these pressures the landlords were able to make a package deal with all of the remaining tenants except three. The landlords then filed a protest designed to eliminate the four-month waiting period. We contested this protest, and the four-month stay was upheld. I then attempted to attack the issuance of the Certificate of Eviction (which would have given us much more than four months), but this move was unsuccessful.

As of December 16, 1971, the landlords had the right to ask for a court order evicting us from the apartment. However, we still had several legal cards to play. We could take the Rent Office to the State Supreme Court and, if we lost, we might be able to appeal the adverse ruling in higher courts. If we lost everywhere in the courts, we knew that judges usually grant an additional waiting period of one to six months if the tenant intends to move but has been unable to find new housing.

In a fourth round of negotiations, I offered to settle for a rental apartment which the landlord had found for us plus keeping money (after taxes) of twenty-five thousand dollars. On August 19, 1971 Mr. Slate called me and told me that the principal landlord ". . . refuses to accede to your demands." I replied that there were now only three tenants in possession of apartments on the entire site. Once the other two tenants agreed to a settlement, failure to reach a settlement with us would begin to cost them thousands of dollars per day. I repeated that we had no intention of penalizing the landlord and no intention of blocking or delaying the project, but that we had no way of settling unless the landlord agreed. I suggested that the principal landlord who had refused to deal with me should reconsider his decision. While he was doing so, the price at which we would be willing to settle would rise by one thousand dollars per calendar day.

At this point, we bought a piano for my daughter and had it moved into our apartment. We realized that the relocator, whose office was located on the ground floor of our building, would soon communicate this fact to our landlords. The effect of moving a piano into a ten-story building in which only three tenants lived can only be conjectured, but we thought it would be helpful.

One of the other two remaining tenants called me and told me that he thought we could make a favorable package deal, emptying the building. I told him that although it was none of my business, I was curious about how much he wanted. Twenty thousand dollars, he said. As the last price the landlord had paid a tenant was sixteen thousand dollars, I told him twenty did not sound too difficult. He then wondered about twenty-five thousand and said he thought he could get us that sum in a package deal. I told him that I wanted to handle our situation myself and that he should not include us in any package offer.

This same tenant called me the next weekend and told me that he had worked out a package deal for the three of us for seventy-five thousand dollars.

"How much of the seventy-five would be ours?" I asked.

After a pause, which indicated that he had been put off by this question, he replied:

"The three of us would share the seventy-five equally. Why, are you any better than I?"

"Not necessarily better, but different. You don't have a genuine offer of seventy-five thousand dollars. They are simply positioning you. As I told you, I intend to handle our situation myself and all I can do is wish you luck with your own situation."

The landlords had broken off negotiations with me on August 19 and I heard nothing further from them for some time. During this interval, I wondered if I had overplayed my hand. Once they settled with the other two tenants, they could begin putting in the foundation of the new building at the far end of the site while working out a legal means of evicting us. If that happened we might get nothing, as the landlords had often threatened.

I decided to seek legal counsel and made an appointment with the alleged tiger for tenants' rights originally suggested to the legal committee of our building.

After keeping me waiting almost an hour, during which time I read of his exploits in various periodicals, the tiger finally invited me into his office. He leafed through the various papers in my file and asked what

I wanted him to do. I replied that I had refused an offer of sixteen thousand dollars (before taxes) plus an apartment our landlords had found for us, and wanted twenty-five thousand (after taxes) plus the apartment. If the landlords found that unacceptable, I wanted somebody good and knowledgeable like himself to appear for us in court. Once we began the proceeding, I was sure the landlords would settle the matter immediately.

He told me that he would handle the case for twenty per cent of the total settlement. When I realized he meant twenty per cent including the sixteen thousand I had already been offered without his assistance, I told him that seemed excessive. I offered to give him twenty per cent above the sixteen thousand dollars, or pay him more than his customary fee to handle the court proceeding, or make some other mutually acceptable arrangement. When he insisted on twenty per cent of the total settlement, I told him that there was no need to take up any more of his time.

The other two tenants settled for a reported twenty-two thousand five hundred dollars, and my family was now the sole holdout. We would be living in the building alone in about two weeks.

On November 11, twelve weeks after our last conversation with the landlord (during which I had many opportunities to wonder whether I had overplayed the hand), I received a telephone call from Mr. Slate.

He told me that the principal landlord accepted our offer.

"Just a moment," I said, making sure he couldn't hear my sigh of relief. "Let me check my calendar. It took him eighty-four days to reach that decision, so I'm adding eighty-four thousand dollars to the price."

"No, damn it. Not including the eighty-four thousand dollars."

"O.K.," said I. "But this time I don't want to see the contract until it's drawn properly."

I then gave him the name and address of an attorney to whom to send the contract.

The agreement with the old landlords was soon reached, but there were still some problems with the new landlord. We had been offered a one-month lease on the new apartment but found that unacceptable. In addition, my daughter had a pet rabbit, some gerbils and a guinea pig, and I wanted them written into the lease, but the new landlord refused to change the "no pets" clause.

"Can you see a judge in this town evicting you because you have a rabbit?" asked Mr. Slate.

"I just don't want to sign any paper where I start out by breaching the contract."

The balance of the negotiations, which we conducted from our suite at the Adams Hotel (with the rabbit), was extremely cordial. The landlord of the new building was rather difficult, but we did get a two-year lease and some minor adjustments plus twenty-five thousand dollars of keeping money from our old landlords. They were so anxious to get rid of us that they picked up our hotel bill for the week prior to relocation and even made some improvements in our new apartment—storm windows, scraping and staining of the floors, painting, and vinyl tiling for the kitchen.

The new apartment is excellent. It has a twenty-one-foot kitchen, a wood-burning fireplace, two full baths, good views on a high floor, an elevator man, and is conveniently located. Although we got more than any of the other tenants, I think it is fair to say that my landlords and I knew I could have doubled our demands and they would have been met.

Now, if they would only co-op our building, we could probably make enough of a profit buying and selling the new apartment to live like grandees in Portugal.

You Go Out of Your Way to Get There . . . Barney's Pays You Back

Barney's, a large clothing store in New York, is rather inconveniently located at Seventh Avenue and Seventeenth Street. The store ran a radio advertising campaign based on the theme that since the customer had to travel to shop at Barney's, the store repaid him with good values.

I decided to buy a few suits at Barney's and arrived there to find sizable crowds milling about on every floor. With some difficulty, I picked out three suits and at last was able to find a vacant dressing room and have them fitted.

A couple of weeks later, I again made the trek to Barney's to pick up the suits. Not a single jacket or pair of pants fit. When I asked to see somebody in authority, Mr. Blue approached—a rather amiable man who thought the problem could be easily remedied. He assured me that if I came back in a few days the suits would fit perfectly. I explained that

I usually bill between a hundred and a hundred and fifty dollars an hour for my time, and that under the best of circumstances it would be difficult to break even transacting business with Barney's. Under the present circumstances, where zero out of six items fit, it seemed extremely unlikely that six out of six would fit on the next go-round. I also told Mr. Blue that three round trips to the store cost me approximately twenty dollars in cab fares, and as the chances of the suits fitting on the next trip were so poor, I would really prefer to try my luck elsewhere.

Mr. Blue then asked me, as what he called a personal favor, to give the store one more chance. Whether or not the suits fit next time, he would see that I was repaid twenty dollars for the cab fares. As I had told him previously that the hour was growing late and I was missing my dinner, Mr. Blue sportingly told me that he would also take me out to dinner the following week if I would only give the store another chance. His good spirits were so infectious that I agreed.

When I arrived the following week and tried on the suits again, a pattern of overcompensation emerged. The pants that had been too short were now too long, the jackets formerly too small were too large, a waist that had been too loose was now too tight. Even Mr. Blue had to admit that none of the suits fit.

"I am really sorry, Mr. Blue. I guess I will have to begin all over again somewhere else. If you don't mind, I'm going to decline your dinner invitation, but I would like to have the twenty dollars for the cab fares."

"Oh, no," said Mr. Blue, his face suddenly clouding. "I told you you could have the cab fares if you bought the suits. If you don't take the suits I can't give you the twenty dollars."

"That's not correct. You told me I would get the twenty dollars for the cab fares whether or not I took the suits."

But Mr. Blue was adamant.

The following day I called the store and asked for Barney's son, a Mr. Fred Pressman, who now runs the store. Fred was not available and remained elusive despite a few tries on my part, so I finally decided to settle for somebody else. I explained that although I had been satisfied at Barney's in the past, I was rather disappointed with Mr. Blue's failure to make good the cab fares, as promised. I had gone out of my way to get to Barney's, but Barney's had not paid me back.

Later that day, I was told that the matter had been discussed with Mr. Brown, one of the senior executives. Mr. Brown had overruled Mr. Blue, and a check for twenty dollars was being mailed out. I thanked the caller and asked him to thank Mr. Brown.

"You see," he told me, "Mr. Brown is superior to Mr. Blue."

"So am I," I replied.

BARNEY'S CLOTHES, INC.   7727
REFUND ACCOUNT
106 SEVENTH AVENUE   NEW YORK, N. Y. 10011

                                            Dec 1 19 72   1-30
                                                          210
PAY
TO THE
ORDER OF   Ralph Charell $20 00

Twenty and 00   DOLLARS
                                    BARNEY'S CLOTHES, INC., REFUND ACCOUNT

     MANUFACTURERS HANOVER
     TRUST COMPANY
     34th St. at Madison Ave., N. Y., N. Y. 10016

                                                      Auth. Sig.

     ⑆0210⑈0030⑆0130 0⑈01503⑈

76

Barney's Revisited

The last time I went to Barney's to try on the three suits, I was wearing a shirt, pants, and overcoat, which had all been bought there. The shirt, a Cardin which had cost twenty-two dollars (plus tax), had been mis-labeled a thirty-five sleeve when, in fact, the sleeve was a thirty-seven. Although the sleeve length looked ridiculous on the increasingly rare occasions I wore it, I hadn't planned to bother returning it. However, as I had to go to Barney's to pick up the suits, I thought I'd show them the shirt at the same time.

When I asked for my money back, the shirt department suggested I instead have the sleeves shortened. To successive layers of the shirt hierarchy, I explained that shortening would be unsatisfactory because it would alter the tapered shape of the sleeves. After spending more time than the shirt was worth, a Mr. Forest Green and I reached an agreement.

The Executive Bonus

I once placed the following ad in the Sunday *New York Times:*

AM I THE MAN YOU WANT
Columbia law graduate, 33, nine yrs. Wall St. doing everything from clerk to president own firm. Am bright, creative, attractive, articulate, untiring, fast, accurate, dependable, a virtual compulsive on details and deadlines and extremely personable. Adapt immediately to new surroundings. Have done creative writing—novel, plays, essays, comedy material, as well as business writing—reports, correspondence, presentations. First-rate with people, problems, words, ideas. Work equally well in vests and buttondowns or shirtsleeves. Consider any job offer except selling. If you think you need

an entire staff to get things done, please
allow me to demonstrate that
I AM THE MAN YOU WANT
X4406 TIMES

I received a number of job offers, including several
sales positions. The first response came from the president of a vitamin pill company, and I arranged to
meet him at his office. He was a rough-hewn, self-
made man who had entered the vitamin business
shortly before pill-popping became a national craze,
and he had prospered. His company called itself the
largest manufacturer of vitamin pills selling directly
to the public. He offered me a job managing five
departments of the company. The salary was not espe-
cially attractive but I accepted the offer, as I had been
living out of capital for almost a year and the job
promised an executive bonus of potentially mythic
(but unspecified) proportions.

The company did about eighty per cent of its business in mail-order vitamins. My five departments,
about 30 employees in all, were concerned with processing the orders, keeping the mail-order lists current
and accurate, writing copy for the catalogs, handling
customer services, and other administrative duties.

Although my staff seemed to be working unceas-
ingly, each day they were a bit farther behind. Cartons
of unfinished work were piled atop one another. A
squad of post-office employees moonlighted at night,
sorting the thousands of IBM cards which the staff

had been unable to handle during the day. In general, the office was a shambles and morale was poor.

In a relatively short period of time, I was able to turn the situation around. Soon the staff was able to handle more than a day's work each day. All of the backlogs disappeared. The postal employees were no longer needed. It became a matter of pride that not even on the busiest days of the year was any work left undone. Morale zoomed.

The company had what it called a premium plan by which customers were given coupons (like trading stamps, but much more valuable) for each dollar's worth of the company's products they purchased. These coupons could be redeemed for a variety of inexpensive houseware items. Approximately one hundred fifty thousand dollars was spent on these gift items each year, and the entire premium plan was administered at no profit to the company. In addition to losses due to pilferage and breakage, the company paid all of the postage and honored sundry complaints about broken merchandise or the failure to receive items with another shipment.

After I had been with the company a few weeks, I realized that the company was missing an important opportunity with the premium plan. In a fairly detailed report which I submitted to the president of the company, I suggested that, in addition to all of the customary gifts, the company should offer the opportunity of converting coupons into the company's products. The company made no profit on the gift items, but a large profit on its pills. At the same time, as the mail-order vitamin business is largely a matter of price, the customers would be extremely receptive to buying the company's products at a slight discount. I estimated that at least seventy-five per cent of the coupons that were converted would be converted into the company's products. This would limit the outlays for the gift items and all of the losses that those items entailed. It would also encourage and stimulate repeat business by virtue of the discount the coupons offered. This would increase the company's volume and profit margins.

From time to time, I asked the president of the company whether he had had an opportunity to study my report. Finally, a meeting was held and the plan was adopted, with me as its administrator. I devised a new coupon, wrote the copy which went into millions of catalogs and put the plan into operation. From the outset, it was an enormous success and exceeded my original estimates.

Toward the end of the year, the president of the company became seriously ill. At Christmas time, one of the vice presidents came to my office and told me that the president of the company wanted me to know that the check for two weeks' salary which he was giving me was only part of the bonus I would be getting, and the balance would be given me when the president was well enough to decide the additional amount each executive should receive.

Shortly after the beginning of the following year,

I accepted another job offer. As I had been with the vitamin company about fifteen months, which included all of the previous year, and had done an excellent job, I knew I had earned the balance of the bonus which had been promised me. When it was not forthcoming, I asked for it. At first I was told to wait; finally, I was informed that I would not be getting any additional bonus from the company.

The president of the company never did return to work. The company was sold to a publicly traded company and, on inquiry, I was again told that I could expect nothing further. I called a friend of mine, a trial lawyer whose successful exploits in court had enthralled me for years.

"Do you have a written contract which specifies the bonus?" he asked me.

"If I did, would I be calling you?"

"Without a contract, you don't have any case."

"I think I do, and if that's your opinion, I'll handle it myself."

For a few dollars, I bought a summons and complaint and had it served on the company. Willkie, Gallagher, Farr, Walton and Fitzgibbon handled the case for the company. I was asked to attend an examination before trial at their office. I suggested that we could save time by my examining the other side at the same time and place and with the same stenographer. Their offices were located at One Chase Manhattan Plaza and I believe they occupied several floors of that building. Near the elevator, and stretching almost as far as the eye could see, were framed paintings of the various members of the firm, beginning with Wendell Willkie.

I was closely questioned for about seventy-five pages of testimony, and then questioned the vice-president who appeared for the vitamin company for about ninety pages. It seemed pretty clear to me that I had established the two classes of bonus (executive and non-executive) and that I was either entitled to an additional sum of money for the balance of the executive bonus or an even larger sum for a great deal of unpaid overtime.

The transcribed testimony looked even better than it had sounded. I was convinced I would have no difficulty proving my case in court. However, as I was about to undergo surgery, I wanted to clear the decks of as many loose ends as possible.

I called the lawyer who was representing the company and told him that when I had put a $2600 price tag on the case I thought that amount might be a bit excessive, but that after reading the testimony I thought it looked within reach. I referred him to a number of pages in which the witness for the company had made the company's side indefensible and told him that for personal reasons I would be willing to settle the entire matter for five hundred dollars but only if I received that amount before the close of business that day. The lawyer told me he would discuss it with his client. Willkie, Gallagher, Farr, Walton and Fitzgibbon were going to go into a huddle with the client on this gigantic five-hundred-dollar case and would get back to me, which they did:

"Four seventy-five," countered the lawyer.

I took that as a joke, but when the lawyer failed to join my laughter, I was puzzled.

"Are you serious?" I asked.

"Yes. I can offer you four seventy-five but no more."

"If I didn't have a personal problem, I wouldn't settle for a penny less than the twenty-six hundred. Four seventy-five is acceptable, but only if it arrives before 5:00 PM today."

The check was delivered within two hours.

A New Friend at Citizens Bank and Trust

In the early stages of my business life I could not maintain the minimum balance required for a regular checking account. For years I paid a small charge for each check I wrote plus a monthly charge to Chase Manhattan. Three thousand one hundred thirty-six checks and scores of monthly fees later (a total of about five hundred dollars), I heard about a little bank in Central Valley, New York, which offered regular checking accounts with no monthly fees, no charges for checks, and no minimum balance required. I switched my account to Central Valley.

A couple of thousand Central Valley Bank checks later, during which time tens of thousands of my dollars had flowed through the bank, I got a notice with one of my statements. The bank's policy had changed. Depositors were to maintain a minimum balance of two hundred dollars or they would be charged a monthly fee.

I called the bank and pointed out that my balances had occasionally exceeded twenty thousand dollars. However, because of the flow of checks and deposits, a particular balance might temporarily dip below two hundred dollars on a rare occasion. I would have thought this account profitable for the bank. Although I certainly was not contesting their new policy, unless its effect was waived with respect to my account, I intended to close the account.

The bank would look into the matter and call me back. When I did not receive the return call after a few days, I called again. I was told that a Mr. Cavanagh was going to watch my account. He would decide later how to handle my request but in the meantime there would be no monthly charge if I failed to maintain the minimum balance. However, they reserved the right to impose the fee at any time without notice.

The following month, I closed this account and opened an account with the Citizens Bank and Trust Company in Chicago, where account holders may write as many free checks as desired against the entire account and receive maximum savings interest, compounded daily, on the remaining balance with no minimum balance required. The bank is in the two-hundred-million-dollar class and the account is insured by the F.D.I.C. In a couple of years I expect to be ahead of the game, despite my erstwhile friend at Chase Manhattan.

March 15, 1973

Dear Customer:

As you may be aware, on March 6, 1973 the merger of The Central Valley National Bank with First National City Corporation was completed resulting in the establishment of Citibank (Mid-Hudson), N.A. with headquarters in Central Valley. Despite the change in name, you should continue to use your present supply of checks and passbooks. When you reorder, your new checks will reflect the change.

We of Citicorp feel very fortunate to have been able to join with a bank of the quality of The Central Valley National Bank and to be able to count on the continuing service of Arthur Cavanagh and his fine staff.

Art and I would like to assure you that nothing has changed except an increased ability to serve you.

Our expansion program is designed to give us the opportunity to serve the individual consumer and the commercial enterprises in Orange, Rockland, Putnam, Dutchess, Sullivan and Ulster Counties.

We feel sure that our new organization will perform in a manner that will continue to merit your confidence and loyalty. Those of us who are new faces to the Mid-Hudson community look forward to meeting you and becoming a part of this, our new home.

Very truly yours,

Harry B. Heneberger, Jr.
President

April 6, 1973

Mr. Arthur Cavanagh
Citibank (Mid-Hudson), N.A.
Route 32
Central Valley, New York 10917

Dear Mr. Cavanagh:

Kindly close my account 2 100169 and send me
a check for my closing balance.

Although I have much enjoyed doing business
with the bank in the past, I see no reason to accept
your recently changed policy with respect to the
requirement of maintaining a minimum balance or
being charged a fee.

During March 1973, owing to the ebb and flow
of deposits and checks, the balances in my account
ranged from more than seven thousand dollars to
less than one hundred dollars. Despite (1) the
thousands of dollars on deposit for much of the·
month and (2) an average daily balance several
times your newly imposed minimum, presumably
constituting a profit-making situation for the
bank, the effect of your new policy would be to
impose a service charge on this account. Thus, I
would be in the anomalous and unacceptable position of being penalized by the company for which
my deposits were creating profits and at the same
time depriving myself of the opportunity to receive
interest on my money and write as many free checks

as I liked without any requirement of a minimum balance, by dealing with other banks.

To suddenly impose this new burden on account holders at a time when there is a growing trend toward removing such fees and even paying interest on similar funds seems penny-wise. Is this new policy in the bank's interest (no pun intended)?

Sincerely,
Ralph Charell

Matching Wits with Dean Witter

My wife and I used to invest and speculate in securities and commodities through Dean Witter and Co., a large brokerage house. Our accounts were easy to service because my wife never communicated with the firm and I simply placed our orders without any counsel from anybody there. Over the course of several years, Dean Witter made a number of small errors in our accounts which seemed too trivial to call to their attention.

In February of 1972, during a lunch hour, I visited my customers' man and placed an order for seven corporate bonds at the market. Although the order was correctly written, the broker erroneously bought nine bonds instead of seven. Two bonds were purchased at 80¾ and seven at 82. In adjusting the order, Dean Witter sent us a cancellation on the two bonds which had been purchased at 80¾.

According to them we had purchased seven bonds at 82.

I told my customers' man that we should have purchased two bonds at 80¾ and five at 82, and (as each point on a bond is worth $10) Dean Witter owed us twenty-five dollars. He agreed with me, and after several weeks (much longer than it should have taken), our account was credited with the twenty-five dollars.

In August of 1972 I entered an open order to sell the seven bonds at 103. The following day I learned that six such bonds had traded at 103 shortly after the market opened. When I asked my customers' man whether any of our bonds had been sold at that price, he told me that he had asked the order clerk that question a number of times with no response. Subsequently, he found out that the open order which had been placed the previous day had not been entered until after he called it to the order clerk's attention.

I asked whether we would have been entitled to sell any of our bonds if the order had been properly entered. An executive at that branch of Dean Witter told me we would have been entitled to sell "some" of our bonds. How many was "some"? Between one and six, I was told. After some further conversation, the company offered to sell our six bonds at the market and credit us the difference between the sale price and 103. This was acceptable to me.

Shortly thereafter, I attempted to place a commodity order with the firm and was informed that no further orders, except liquidating orders, would be accepted in any of our accounts. My surprise and indignation were undisguised and after much protest, the restriction was relaxed somewhat and I was permitted to enter an order straddling our position in potatoes. (As we were short of May potatoes, this allowed us to buy an equal number of contracts of March potatoes.) However, when that order was delayed so long that we lost more than three hundred dollars, and when the firm repeatedly disavowed any liability, the correspondence began.*

The facts were simply set forth. Because of an office rule, of which I was unaware, requiring the manager's approval of all commodity orders of ten or more contracts, our market order was delayed for more than ten minutes while our customers' man searched in vain for the manager. Finally, in response to my repeated objections, the customers' man got the approval of a different executive and the order was entered. However, because of the fluctuations in price during the delay, we paid over three hundred dollars more than we would have if the order had been entered at once. I wrote to the New York Mercantile Exchange, setting forth these facts, but got nowhere. I decided to present the matter to the chairman and president of the brokerage house.

*On the theory that "them that has, gets," I recommend one use the best personal stationery one can afford. I use Tiffany & Co.'s ecru with a kid finish and dark brown ink.

September 8, 1972

Mr. William M. Witter
Chairman, Dean Witter & Co., Inc.
45 Montgomery Street
San Francisco, California 94016

Dear Mr. Witter:

My wife and I have had accounts at a branch office of Dean Witter for several years. For the past several months the volume of errors in these accounts have multiplied to the point that we have learned to expect to spend several hours each month trying to make sense of the various statements we receive. It is a fact that scores of errors have been committed by the firm.

Because I attempted to correct some of the errors admittedly committed by Dean Witter with no fault whatever on my part, Mr. Magenta, the branch manager, informed me that my account was unwelcome and that no orders in my accounts would be acceptable under any circumstances, except liquidating orders. Mr. Magenta reached this decision without ever having discussed the matter with me, without ever having met me, and, indeed, without much of a grasp of the facts.

Subsequently, I met with Mr. Magenta who told me that the matter was closed. As there were two somewhat costly errors in question at the time, I attempted to discuss the matter with Mr. Yellow. Mr. Yellow left for vacation and I never heard from him again. I called Mr. Orchid on a number of occasions. Mr. Orchid was either not at his desk or was otherwise occupied, and he did not return a single telepnone call. I was therefore under some pressure to discuss the matter with Mrs. Gray, despite the fact that this course appeared difficult and unavailing because of her hostile attitude.

At this point, the only open item involves ten contracts of New York March potatoes. Despite the fact that the material facts I have alleged have been admitted by the customers' man and these admissions have been heard in a conference call and taken down verbatim with the knowledge and permission of Mrs. Gray and Mr. Vermilion, Mrs. Gray has decided that the firm has no liability.

Therefore, the matter has been respectfully brought to the attention of the Chairman and the President of the firm. If, after a reasonable interval, we do not reach a mutually satisfactory resolution, I will move the matter into appropriate federal agencies, reserving all of my rights, in the unlikely event that these avenues should prove unavailing.

This matter is but one small part of the surface of a situation which cries out for correction. I would be pleased to meet with you or your representatives in person and at once in an effort to examine this situation.

Sincerely,
Ralph Charell

cc: Mr. G. Willard Miller, President

September 15, 1972

Mr. William M. Witter
Chairman, Dean Witter & Co., Inc.
45 Montgomery Street
San Francisco, California 94016

Dear Mr. Witter:

Further to my letter of September 8, the following:

Recently, New York May potatoes opened down the limit and I attempted to cover four contracts. I will not take your time to go into the manner in which these orders were handled except to say that they were handled in a manner totally unsatisfactory to me. Whether or not the errors and delays involved actually damaged us I honestly do not know and do not intend to pursue, although it is clear that the methods of entering commodity orders in that office are totally unacceptable. With the help of Mr. Aquamarine, my commodity account is in the process of being transferred to Merrill Lynch and this source of irritation, unhappiness, financial loss, etc., will, hopefully, soon be discontinued.

Some further checking indicates that stocks which I had requested be transferred as of July 12, 1972 and which, according to Mrs. Gray and others, had been taken care of some weeks ago, actually (again according to Mrs. Gray) went into transfer on August 31. This, despite the assurances of Mrs.

Gray and others that the stock had been put into transfer as long ago as July 15. There has been a rather consistent pattern in our accounts of undue delay in the delivery of stocks and checks.

I am enclosing a confirmation of an open order which is part of my file, since it is the best quickly understood piece of tangible evidence of the kind of nightmarish lack of competence we have experienced. This one small item contains no fewer than *six* errors.

1. My first name is misspelled.
2. This order (and the bonds) were in the joint account and they omitted this fact and my wife's name.
3. The zip code is 10021 not 10028.
4. My account number is 35460 not 34980.
5. The coupon is 5-1/4 not 5-1/2.
6. The maturity date is 82 not 92.

Whether or not you care to look into the management of the office in question is somewhat peripheral (although not entirely irrelevant) to my principal concerns. First, I would like some expression as to whether or not Mr. Magenta acted properly in forbidding any but liquidating orders in any of our accounts simply because I attempted to correct some of the more costly errors committed by the firm through no fault of ours. Second, now that Mr. Vermilion has admitted the facts and these admissions have been heard by Mrs. Gray and my secretary and me and have been taken down verbatim (with the permission of Mrs. Gray and Mr. Vermilion) an appropriate adjustment would seem to be overdue.

The facts are clear. Any self-serving allegations that may be made at this point are of little consequence. I have spent a good deal more time than should have been necessary to correct this situation. The amount of time spent and Mrs. Gray's rather undisguised hostility have become increasingly irksome and tiresome.

Certainly, I do not wish to take up a great deal of your time with this matter. Therefore, I have decided, in fairness to all of us, that if we cannot reach a mutually satisfactory adjustment on this trade as well as an expression with respect to Mr. Magenta's hasty and ill-conceived actions, I intend to forward a copy of my entire file (including all of the errors made on my statements, the federal rules that were violated, etc.) to the S.E.C. and C.E.A. I see no reason to carry this outrageous and unjust burden any farther without outside help.

Sincerely,
Ralph Charell

Enclosure
cc: Mr. G. Willard Miller, President

DEAN WITTER & Co.
INCORPORATED

MEMBER NEW YORK STOCK EXCHANGE

11401-4 (414M-1/71)

MR. RALPHA CHARELL   *MRS JULIANNE CHARELL*

NEW YORK, NEW YORK 10028   -3

8-3-72   85-34980-1-M-67

SL 1M GRAY MFG. 5½-92 @ 103

58

DEAN WITTER & CO.

SAN FRANCISCO
LOS ANGELES

INCORPORATED

NEW YORK
CHICAGO

MEMBER • NEW YORK STOCK EXCHANGE, INC.

45 MONTGOMERY STREET • SAN FRANCISCO, CALIFORNIA 94106

TELEPHONE (415) 392-7211

September 25, 1972

Mr. Ralph Charell
~~————————————~~
New York, NY ~~————~~

Dear Mr. Charell:

Mr. William Witter has asked me to respond to your letter of September 15, 1972.

I am sorry that you believe you were damaged because Mr. Baker sought to obtain approval before entering your order to buy ten New York March potatoes on August 8. However, Mr. Baker has acted properly because we have a house rule which requires the branch manager's approval in the case of any commodity orders involving ten units or more. This rule is for the customer's protection.

Notwithstanding the above, since you are obviously distressed because of the short delay in executing this order, we are willing to credit you with the difference between the price that could have been obtained for ten units of March potatoes at the opening on August 8 and the price you actually paid.

I am doing this in the spirit of settling this dispute and it should not be construed to be an admission of liability on our part. At the opening on August 8, six units of March potatoes were trading in the range of 4.40 to 4.41. Actually, only one of the lots traded at 4.40 and the other five traded at 4.41. In addition, eight lots traded at 4.41 at 10:06 a.m.

In view of the above, we are willing to give you a credit as if your first lot traded at 4.40 and the balance traded at 4.41. I calculate that this would give you a credit of $335.00.

102

Mr. Ralph Charell   -2-   September 25, 1972

        If you are in agreement with my proposal I would appreciate it if you
would execute and have notarized at least one copy of the enclosed release and return
that copy to me (the second copy is for your own records). Upon receipt of the
executed release I will cause a check in the amount of $335.00 to be sent to you.

                        Very truly yours,

                        Olive Drab, Esq.

Enclosures

cc: Light Mauve
     Medium Magenta
     Dark Gray

DEAN WITTER & CO.

INCORPORATED

MEMBER · NEW YORK STOCK EXCHANGE, INC.

45 MONTGOMERY STREET • SAN FRANCISCO, CALIFORNIA 94106

TELEPHONE (415) 392-7211

September 29, 1972

Mr. Ralph Charell

New York, NY

Dear Mr. Charell:

I herewith enclose our check in the amount of $335.00 payable to you and your wife. This check represents the difference between the price that could have been obtained for ten units of March potatoes at the opening of the market on August 8 and the price you paid.

Please acknowledge receipt of this check by signing the enclosed copy of this letter and returning it in the self-addressed envelope.

Very truly yours,

Olive Drab, Esq.

Enclosures

More to See on Cable TV

A pile of four-page circulars appeared in the lobby of our apartment building one day. In big, bold letters the front page announced: HERE IS OUR OFFER TO YOU: A WHOLE SUMMER OF CABLE TV SERVICE FREE!

The circular explained that if we accepted the cable TV service, the charges for the summer months would be waived and the installation charges would be postponed until fall. My wife and I decided to accept the offer, and cable was installed on two of our television sets.

Almost immediately, contrary to the terms of the offer, we were billed $27.90 (a monthly charge of six dollars for the first set, two dollars for the second set plus installation charges of nine ninety-five per set). I called Sterling Manhattan Cable Television, Inc. and explained the problem. I was assured that the company would cancel this bill and begin to bill us in September. The following month I received a notice dunning me for an account "sixty days past due" and threatening a "late processing charge . . . if you do not remit promptly. Thank you."

I again called Sterling and explained that this matter was to have been taken care of the previous month. I was told that the records would be checked and someone from the company would get back to me. When the call came, a Sterling employee explained that he was sorry I was being dunned but that, after all, I did owe that amount at this time (since the

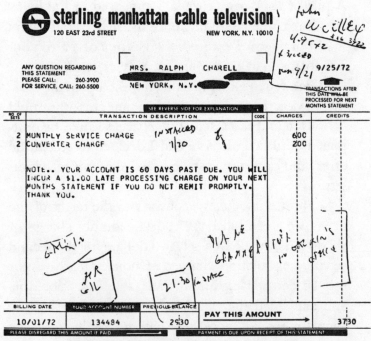

summer was now over) and he would appreciate my remitting the total amount as soon as possible so that he could remove my account from the past due file. His manner was distasteful.

After noting that I usually bill between a hundred and a hundred and fifty dollars an hour for my time and that it was difficult to see how I could break even on this transaction, I explained that the proposed solution of my immediately paying the full amount was unacceptable and that a bill like this one, which did not include an opening date and a closing date for the billing, was an anachronism, at best. In addition, the front page of the circular had stated that the subscriber would be entitled to an entire summer of free service and as the summer did not end until September 21 (not September 1), I would expect to be billed from that date. Furthermore, it was only about five hundred words of copy later (if one got that far) that one was informed that there would be any installation charges. In view of these deficiencies and the time I had put into trying to correct their errors, I stated that I would be willing to be billed from September 21, without any installation charges, and would be happy to pay such a corrected bill within one day of its receipt. I also wondered aloud whether there actually was such a person as the "Shirley Jones" who had signed her name in the circular.

After some conversation a Mr. Royal Blue came on the line. I was absolutely correct, he said, the billing system was faulty and he would be happy to correct my bill so that I would be billed from September 21. It was illegal, he told me, for Sterling not to charge for installation, but instead of nine ninety-five for each set, the installation charge to me would be four ninety-five per set. I replied that although I was somewhat curious as to precisely which statute would be contravened by not charging for installation, his proposed solution was acceptable, and I thanked Mr. Blue.

A couple of weeks later, instead of being billed as agreed, I received a letter from one of Sterling's vice presidents (see facing page).

I called Mr. Yellow and asked him whether he was aware of the agreement Mr. Blue and I had reached concerning my account. He replied in the affirmative. I told him that surprised me because he had failed to mention the agreement when he unilaterally decided to breach it with his letter of October 19. I told him that if the agreement was not honored, I would not require Sterling's services. I gave Mr. Yellow until the close of business that day to make up his mind whether to honor my agreement with Mr. Blue. If he did not, I would take the matter up with the appropriate person in the parent company.

Mr. Yellow attempted to question me on each of the points he had outlined in his letter. I replied that I was sorry to discontinue the conversation, but as I usually billed between a hundred and a hundred and fifty dollars an hour for my time, I wanted to spend as little of it as I could on a matter of this

STERLING MANHATTAN CABLE TELEVISION, INC.
A Sterling Communications company
120 East 23 Street, New York 10010 (212) 260-3900

October 19, 1972

Mr. Ralph Charell
████████████
New York, N.Y.

Dear Mr. Charell:

Regarding problems you have had with understanding our
billing system, the following will be done:

    1) Your account will be credited so that, in effect,
       your service charges begin as of September 1, 1972
       as stated in our printed September billing cir-
       cular.

    2) Your installation charges will be $9.95 for each
       set as stated in our printed September billing
       circular.

    3) This means that your November 1 bill will be as
       follows:

$9.95	Installation of 1 set.
9.95	Installation of 2nd set.
8.00	September
8.00	October
8.00	November (one month in advance
	November 1 to November 30).
$43.90	Total

Following up another of your questions, we assure you that
Shirley Jones does indeed exist.

Thank you for taking the time to let us know about your problems
with our billing system.

Very truly yours,

Chrome Yellow
Vice President

small scale. I told him the choice was entirely his and I was sure he could reach the appropriate decision, which he did later that day.

X-Rays

My wife, Julianne, had some pain in her back and decided to go to a chiropractor. Before he treated her, the chiropractor recommended that X-rays be taken and referred her to an X-ray laboratory. When Julianne asked the chiropractor to suggest the best person at the laboratory to take the X-rays, he named a Dr. Pink.

I accompanied my wife to the laboratory at the appointed time. The receptionist recorded a few facts, which Julianne supplied, on an index card and informed us that the lab required payment in advance. We thought that was unusual, as we had always been billed for medical services in the past. The receptionist explained that it was nothing personal, merely an inflexible policy of the laboratory. When Julianne asked how much the payment would be, the receptionist responded by asking her what sort of medical coverage she had. Armed with this information, the receptionist conferred with a young man with a Fu Manchu moustache and then replied that the X-rays would be one hundred twenty-five dollars.

"One hundred twenty-five dollars for a few X-rays?" I asked. "Doesn't that sound a bit exorbitant?"

I was told that the hundred twenty-five dollars covered the X-rays plus the time their people spent marking the X-rays for interpretation. The explanation was unconvincing, but as my wife was in pain and we had already invested a certain amount of time in the procedure, I wrote a check for one hundred twenty-five dollars, got a receipt, and asked to see Dr. Pink. The receptionist told me that Dr. Pink was not present.

"But we made an appointment to see Dr. Pink this morning," I persisted.

"Dr. Pink doesn't *take* the X-rays. Dr. Pink *interprets* them," I was told.

Although my wife and I thought that Dr. Pink had been recommended as the man to take the X-rays, there was room for the slightest doubt. With misgivings, we accepted the explanation and Julianne had the X-rays taken by the young man with the Fu Manchu moustache.

Over the following weekend I noticed that the receipt I had been given had been stamped with the name of another doctor, not that of Dr. Pink. As the receptionist's explanation had never been completely satisfactory and as the name of Dr. Pink, as well as his person, had been mysteriously absent from the entire procedure, I called the laboratory and asked to speak with Dr. Pink.

"Dr. Pink speaking." His voice was artificially pitched low enough to be that of the average funeral director.

I explained that my wife and I had been recommended by my wife's chiropractor and that I had a couple of brief questions which would require a bit of clarification.

"Come and see me," said Dr. Pink. "If you want to talk to me you will have to come and see me."

"There's no need to spend that much time," said I. "We can handle the entire matter in a couple of minutes right now."

"Come and see me," repeated Dr. Pink.

"The only reason I am speaking with you at all, Dr. Pink, is that I want to be fair by including some inputs from you before I call the New York County Medical Society."

"Well, what is it?" he relented.

I explained that we had been recommended to him for taking the X-rays as well as interpreting them. Payment in advance had been demanded, and before the amount had been fixed we had been asked about our medical insurance coverage. I told Dr. Pink that I believed we were overcharged, that I had discovered that he did take X-rays, and that another doctor had interpreted the X-rays at that laboratory.

Dr. Pink asserted that the entire procedure seemed

quite unexceptional to him and that he could not understand the basis of our claim. I told him that I intended to get an estimate for the X-rays from the first five companies which would answer the question from among those listed under the same heading in the yellow pages as his laboratory and promised to get back to him later that day with the results of my inquiries. At that point, if we could not agree on a fair price, I intended to go a great deal farther.

A few phone calls told me that the average price for this series of X-rays was about fifty dollars. I then called the New York County Medical Society and spoke with an appropriate executive. Without mentioning any names, I explained the facts. I pointed out that we had been charged more than double the standard price and that this was done only after the extent of our medical coverage had been ascertained. I stated that the price seemed exorbitant and the circumstances outrageous.

"A chiropractor? We don't have anything to do with chiropractors. We regard those people as cultists."

"I have no grievance whatever with the cultist," I explained. "The cultist merely recommended a medical doctor. It is with the medical doctor that our complaint lies."

The Medical Society executive agreed with me that the price seemed excessive and suggested that if I wrote a letter to the committee on ethics and outlined my allegations, the entire matter would be reviewed.

I thanked the executive and said that if I were unable to settle the matter with the doctor I would do precisely that.

As promised, I called Dr. Pink and told him what had taken place. I pointed out that I had, of course, not mentioned any names up to that point. Under the circumstances, I told him, unless we received a check in the amount of seventy-five dollars within two days, I intended to request the intercession of the New York County Medical Society.* After a pregnant pause, Dr. Pink replied:

"And if you do get a check for seventy-five dollars?"

"In that case," said I, "I would consider the entire matter closed."

That evening, when my wife went to see the "cultist," he gave her Dr. Pink's check, delivered earlier by messenger, in the amount of seventy-five dollars.

*For those people who think I might have been somewhat harsh with Dr. Pink (hopefully, only a few), I should point out that I could have stopped payment on the check and dealt with Dr. Pink from a different position. But I regard such tactics as unfair and have never stopped payment on any of the several thousand checks I have written.

The Mark of Excellence

On my way to lunch one day, I walked north on Madison Avenue. As I passed the construction site of the new General Motors building I was suddenly struck with large drops of cement which had fallen from dozens of stories above. Other passersby and the windshields of passing cars were also being splattered. When I looked up to see who might be responsible for the damages, I was struck squarely on the forehead by a tiny piece of stone which had fallen from a great height.

I got through lunch with my hair, suit and shoes encrusted with cement but, happily, no pain in the forehead. After lunch, I called the George B. Fuller Company, the primary contractor at the construction site, and explained what had occurred. I said that as I assumed I had no permanent physical injuries and since the shoes and suit were not new, I would be willing to provide them with a general release for the entire matter at an extremely nominal two hundred dollars—but only if it could be done at once and without my spending any additional time on the matter as I usually bill between. . .

The Fuller man was most understanding.

Later that day, a claims adjuster called and quickly agreed to settle the matter for two hundred dollars. However, it would be necessary for a medical doctor of my own choice to examine me and substantiate the lack of physical injuries. I explained that it wasn't worth my time to do this for such a nominal settlement and that we could save that time by settling the matter on the basis of property damage alone. A general release would also protect them from any later claims with respect to the physical injury. Nevertheless, the man insisted on a note from a doctor.

I arranged to see a doctor on my way home from the office. He located the almost nonexistent laceration and agreed to furnish the note.

When I called the insurance man, note in hand, I told him that I had spent an additional twenty-five dollars for the doctor's services and was adding that amount to the claim. The claims adjuster unreasonably refused. Although this was not an intelligent decision and one that could have, at a minimum, tripled the settlement if I'd wanted to press the claim, I accepted it. Besides, I was beginning to believe that my time was worth at least a hundred to a hundred fifty dollars an hour.

The Magic Carpet

One evening my mother-in-law told my wife and me about her adventures purchasing a rug. Macy's had advertised a warehouse rug sale including one particularly large one reduced to forty-nine dollars, a tiny fraction of its former price. My mother-in-law needed a rug for the extremely large hallway in her huge, old-fashioned apartment on New York's West Side, and she thought that this sale-priced rug could be cut to fit it perfectly. She went out to the warehouse near the close of business on the day before the sale was to begin and tried to buy it, but was told that the sale started the following day and no rugs could be sold before then.

The next morning she waited outside the warehouse until a bell rang signaling its opening. Because she had been there the previous day, she knew precisely where to find the rug she wanted. She entered the first elevator after everybody else so she would be the first person out. This doughty individualist was thus able to beat all the other customers to the large rug and immediately offered to buy it for forty-nine dollars.

The salesman told her it had already been sold and that it was so ticketed.

My mother-in-law objected. She explained that she had come to the warehouse before it closed the previous day and had been told she could not purchase it until the sale day. She had been the first person to arrive that morning, and it seemed odd that somebody else could have already purchased it. The salesman offered a lame explanation.

My mother-in-law persevered. She found a man with a little white flower in his buttonhole and told him the story. There was nothing he could do, he said. If the ticket said "sold," the rug was sold.

She found another man with a white flower in his buttonhole and explained that she had wanted the large rug because she could have had it cut to fit her long hallway and a smaller rug would not do. This man was sympathetic and told my mother-in-law that if she picked out another large rug that was not on sale, he would have it marked down to forty-nine dollars.

However, when the rug was never delivered and much checking revealed that it "had been lost," my mother-in-law went to see the head of the rug department at the main New York store. He heard her complaint and offered her the return of her money but not another rug.

When I heard this story at dinner one evening,

I asked my mother-in-law if she would mind my calling the store.

The following morning I did so and told the head rug man with whom my mother-in-law had spoken that as his time and mine were extremely valuable, I would summarize the story and if he agreed that there was a just grievance here, I would expect him to put things right immediately. He listened to the story again and this time agreed that my mother-in-law had a reasonable complaint. I asked him to call her at once and invite her to pick out a suitable rug that very day.

My mother-in-law is now the proud owner of an avocado green, two-hundred-dollar rug for which she paid forty-nine dollars. Cut to fit her long hallway, the rug is perfect.

Moving Day

After reaching an agreement with our former landlord to vacate our apartment, I arranged for a reputable moving company to move us out on the day after
the agreements were due to be signed. However, a
slight snag delayed the signing and I had to cancel
the moving date. I attempted to reset the date but
the mover could not accommodate us.

Because I knew each day of delay in our moving
might cause the landlord substantial losses, I told him
that we would allow him to make the packing and
moving arrangements for us. We would approve any
first-rate moving company, and would pay the first
seven hundred fifty dollars toward the cost. Our landlord was anxious to get us out as soon as possible
and readily proposed Morgan and Brother Manhattan
Storage Co., Inc. This was acceptable to us. I had
asked for one hundred thousand dollars of insurance
to cover the move, but when the landlord argued that

it was extremely unlikely that the moving company would totally destroy everything we owned, I agreed to twenty thousand dollars of coverage. The premium was $5 per $1000 coverage, or $100.

Two packers arrived one morning and spent the entire day wrapping and packing our goods. The next day the two packers completed the job and four movers loaded the contents of our apartment onto a van and transferred them to the new address. The two packers, now unpackers, unpacked most of the goods. I tipped the six men and they left.

While the packers were completing their part of the job and the movers were in process of loading our goods onto the van, the demolition of the building suddenly began. Almost directly below our apartment (we lived on the second floor) wreckers were plowing a hole about ten feet wide and five feet high into the building. The chandeliers began to sway. The moving people told my wife that unless the demolition stopped immediately, they would walk off the job. She ran downstairs and told the wreckers that there were still people inside who would not be out for a couple of hours. She then called the landlord and the demolition halted until she and the moving men left.

When we finally unpacked I totaled up the various damages and called the moving company. We were supplied with a claim form:

January 10, 1972

Mr. Pale Lavender
Morgan and Brother Manhattan Storage Co.
1411 Third Avenue
New York, New York 10028

Dear Mr. Lavender:

Thank you for your letter of December 20, 1971.

Enclosed is my claim form and some supporting exhibits.

We were very much surprised and disappointed with the lack of care exhibited in this relocation, having dealt with your company previously. For example, your men unsuccessfully attempted to jam the piano into the *passenger* elevator, causing much unnecessary damage, when the freight elevator was available and would have served easily and without damage. No protective pads were used on the piano and your men scampered all over it and subsequently lifted it and rested it on its side.

With respect to those items alleged to be damaged beyond repair, this opinion is that of Murray Hill Radio Television Lab Co. at 1440 Third Avenue.

I am holding the damaged items for the inspection of anybody you may designate and would much appreciate your immediate attention to processing this claim.

Sincerely,
Ralph Charell

STATEMENT OF LOSS AND DAMAGE

RALPH CHARELL   1|8|72
(Name of Claimant)   (Date)

▓▓▓▓▓▓▓▓▓▓▓▓
(Address of Claimant)

NEW YORK, N.Y. ▓▓▓▓ Telephone # ▓▓▓▓

Total value of entire shipment..... $20,000 ..... Cause of damage ▓▓▓▓▓▓▓▓▓▓

Date shipment was loaded ... 12|15|71 ..... Date unloaded 12/17/71

Location from which removed ▓▓▓▓▓▓▓▓▓ — N.Y., N.Y. ▓▓▓▓▓

If claim is for breakage or shortage to items packed in containers give following information:

By whom packed................By whom unpacked................Date unpacked 12/17/71

                                           OUR FAMILY & YOURS TOO

When was damage or shortage discovered DURING UNPACKING ..... By whom.

DETAILED STATEMENT SHOWING HOW AMOUNT CLAIMED IS DETERMINED

(LIST NUMBER, DESCRIPTION OF ITEMS, NATURE AND EXTENT OF LOSS OR DAMAGE, ETC.)	WEIGHT	DATE ACQUIRED	ORIG. COST	AMOUNT NOW CLAIMED
6 CHINA HORSES + 2 HAND-CARVED WOODEN HORSES BROKEN		LESS THAN 6 YRS AGO	6 ▓▓ 2×49	▓
COLOR TELEVISION - A ZENITH TV SET SCRATCHED + MISSING JOINTS, SHATTERED PANEL, DENT ▓ ALTERED TREAD AFFECTED	2 YRS AGO	▓ 350 ▓ SET	▓ 67.27 ▓
PIANO SCRATCHED, SCRAPED, SURFACE CHIP ▓▓ AWAY-NO PARTS ▓▓▓▓▓▓▓ ▓▓▓ ▓▓▓▓ ▓▓▓	A YEAR AGO	6 SET	$75.00 ▓
DRESSER ▓▓▓▓▓ R. CHIPPED + SCRATCHED IN SEVERAL SPOTS	2 YRS AGO	6 SET	53 EST.
FISH TANK SMASHED	FISH ▓▓	▓/10	$10 ▓▓
TYPEWRITER (IBM ELECTRIC) DAMAGED (SEE REPAIR)	▓▓▓ 8 YRS AGO	▓ 175.	▓ 17.05
▓▓▓▓▓▓ ▓▓▓ ▓▓▓▓ P.▓▓▓▓ ▓▓▓) REPAIR - ▓▓▓▓▓▓ ▓▓▓ ▓▓▓▓ ▓▓▓▓	▓▓▓ 10 YRS AGO	▓▓ SET	▓
GARRARD TURNTABLE + SPEAKER DAMAGED BEYOND REPAIR - ▓▓▓ ▓▓▓ ▓▓▓▓	▓▓▓ AGO	▓▓ SET	▓▓▓▓
CUPBOARD FURNITURE SCRATCHED	1 YEAR	$10	▓/10
▓▓▓▓ WATER PRICE LEG ▓▓ ▓▓ OFF + WOOD SPLIT - ▓▓▓▓ TABLE	▓▓▓▓▓▓ 5 YRS.	▓▓ $70	▓ 75
MISC. BOTTLES OF PERFUME SMASHED)		▓▓▓	$5.00

The following documents should be submitted in support of claim ▓▓▓▓▓▓

1. A repairman's estimate of cost of repair. ▓▓▓▓▓▓▓▓▓▓▓▓▓

2. Other papers, documents, etc., in support of the claim, including paid freight bill and bill of lading if not previously surrendered to carrier. ▓▓▓▓▓▓▓▓

                   Ralph Charell
                   Signature of Claimant

Instructions: Please complete, attach documents requested, sign and return:

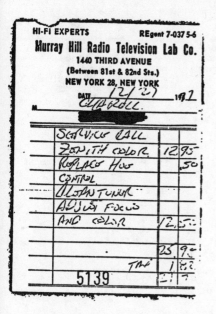

HI-FI EXPERTS   REgent 7-037 5-6

Murray Hill Radio Television Lab Co.
1440 THIRD AVENUE
(Between 81st & 82nd Sts.)
NEW YORK 28, NEW YORK

DATE 12/27 1972

M Charell

SERVICE CALL		
ZENITH COLOR	12	95
REPLACE HUE		50
CONTROL		
ALIGN TUNER		
ADJUST FOCUS		
AND COLOR	12	50
	25	95
TAX	1	82
	27	77

5139

DURING SHIPMENT
THE HUE CONTROL WAS
BROKEN. FOCUS AND
COLOR CONTROLS ON
THE REAR OF THIS SET
WERE MOVED OUT OF
ALIGNMENT

IBM

REMIT TO: P. O. Box 209, New York, New York 10010
INQUIRE AT: 555 Madison Avenue, New York, New York 10022. 223-2500

5238210 — 26N

PROD.	SERIAL	SERVICE HOURS	PHONY T-ELEM	QUAN.	PARTS NAME	TOTAL PRICE
11	011911502	6/10			Backspace bellcrank clamped and repaired	
					Carriage return release link broken and replaced	

INVOICE NUMBER

CUSTOMER NAME
Mr. R. Charell

ADDRESS

CITY STATE   ZIP
New York N.Y.

CUSTOMER REFERENCE

CUSTOMER SIGNATURE
X R. Charell

FEDL.	SERVICE CODE C	B. O. INVOICE	TRAVEL HOURS 2/10		M/A SOLD NC	TOTAL PARTS

MINIMUM REGULAR GUARANTEE

5238210 — 26N

SERVICE CODE 6/10	TOTAL BILLABLE HOURS	X LABOR RATE PER HOUR $ 16 50	TOTAL LABOR 16 50

IBM OFFICE PRODUCTS DIVISION

MAINTENANCE AGREEMENT
ASSURES TOP PERFORMANCE

INVOICE NUMBER

MILES AT ___ EACH, PLUS ___ OTHER EXPENSE =

STATE TAX	COUNTY TAX	CITY TAX .115	TOTAL TAX 1 15

12-25-71   A. Liccu   35984

SERVICE DATES   IBM REPRESENTATIVE SIGNATURE   SERIAL

PLEASE RETURN DUPLICATE
OR INVOICE STUB WITH THIS
AMOUNT

TERMS—NET CASH 30 DAYS

TOTAL AMOUNT 17 65

LABOR GUARANTEE 10 DAYS   PARTS GUARANTEE 90 DAYS

140-0073-16

IT IS HEREBY CERTIFIED THAT THESE GOODS WERE PRODUCED OR THE SERVICES PERFORMED IN COMPLIANCE WITH ALL APPLICABLE REQUIREMENTS OF SECTIONS 6, 7, AND 12 OF THE FAIR LABOR STANDARDS ACT, AS AMENDED, AND OF REGULATIONS AND ORDERS OF THE UNITED STATES DEPARTMENT OF LABOR ISSUED UNDER SECTION 14 THEREOF.

THIS IS YOUR INVOICE

MORGAN AND BROTHER MANHATTAN STORAGE COMPANY, INC.

MOVING
PACKING
STORAGE
FIREPROOF VAULTS

1411 THIRD AVENUE AT 80ᵀᴴ STREET   NEW YORK, N.Y. 10028 · (212) 535-9100
CABLE ADDRESS, MORGANWARE

January 19th, 1972

Mr. Ralph Charell

New York, New York

[handwritten annotation: THE LAW DISTINGUISHES MERELY NEGLIGENT FUNCTIONS & MALFUNCTION WHEN COUPLED WITH PHYSICAL INJURIES]

Dear Mr. Charell:

This is to acknowledge a visit to your home regarding
a claim resulting from your recent removal from 57 East
88th Street to your present address.

We have reviewed your claim with the insurance company
and the executive officers of our Company and wish to
alert you as to liability and settlement of your claim.

With regard to the damaged china horses and wooden
horses, our packer Mr. John Parnahay states,"he did
not pack these items, only packed plastic horses"and
the insurance company has declined liability.

With regard to the damaged television set shown to me
on my visit in the living room, the Company has rejected
liability having not been given the opportunity to inspect
same prior to repairs. However, on the portion which was
shown as damaged, the loosened panel, this has been accepted
as per Peter Lightstone's estimate of $5.00.

With respect to the damaged Piano, responsibility has
been accepted at half of $65.00 based on Mr. Lightstone's
estimate. It is noted before removal from your former
residence, the Piano was listed as chipped, scratched and
marred. Our liability $32.50.

With respect to the damaged Dresser, responsibility has
been accepted at $15.00 transit damages only. The Dresser
is also noted before removal as been chipped, scratched
and marred. And after viewing same, it would appear the
Dresser has been chewed away by an animal of some sort.

With regard to the Fish tank reported broken packer John
Parnahay notes this item was broken upon unpacking and
responsibility has been accepted as per claim forms $10.00.

(continued)

OVER 100 YEARS OF SERVICE   MEMBER Allied Van Lines

128

With respect to the damaged typewriter reported by you
on your forms, liability has been denied since we were
not given the opportunity to inspected same prior to repairs.
Also, the Company will not be responsible for the mechanical
functions of pianos, radios, phonographs, clocks, barometers,
mechanical refrigerators or other instruments or appliances
whether or not such articles are packed or unpacked by the
Company.

With regard to the damaged cupboard Turntable, as shown
on your claim forms, liability has been accepted by the
Company at $10.00 for the damaged ones.

With respect to the damaged Heritage table, since it
is noted by Mrs. Charell, one leg was already broken
off before our men handled same, liability has been
accepted on the other leg based on the estimate at $15.00.

With regard to the damaged medicine bottles as noted on
your claim forms, liability has been accepted by the Company
and a cash settlement alloted for $8.00.

With respect to the damages to the Garrard turntable and
Speaker, responsibility has been denied since the Company
is not responsible for the mechanical functions of appliances
or intruments.

Please find enclosed our Releases in the amount of $90.50,
in full settlement of all claims. Kindly sign these documents
and return same to this office. If it is your desire to have
Mr. Lightstone complete repairs kindly let us know in order
that we may have our check for $67.50 drawn and made payable
to Mr. Lightstone and the balance of $23.00 made payable to you.

We certainly regret there was cause for complaint covering
your shipment, and that we could not honor your claim as fully
as presented, we do trust however, you see the reason for our
position.

Very truly yours,

MORGAN-MANHATTAN
Storage Company, Inc.

Pale Lavender
Customer Service Department

129

<u>RELEASE</u>

KNOW ALL MEN BY THESE PRESENTS

That (we)
~~XXX~~
(1)   MR. RALPH CHARELL

for and in consideration of REPAIRS   Dollars $ __67.50__

"   "   "   "   " REPLACEMENT   Dollars $ __23.00__

"   "   "   "   " CASH   Dollars $ _____

"   "   "   "   "   Dollars $ _____

TOTAL SETTLEMENT $ __90.50__

subject to payment, to release and discharge and by these presents do for,
myself, my heirs, executors, administrators and assigns, release and for-
ever discharge   MORGAN AND BROTHER MANHATTAN STORAGE COMPANY, INC.
         and   ATLANTIC MUTUAL INSURANCE COMPANY

from any and all claims or demands by reason of my recent removal on or

about the ____17th____ day of __DECEMBER_____, 19 __71__

from __New York, New York____ to ____New York, New York____ ,   ,
which I, my heirs, executors, administrators, or assigns can, shall or
may have any reason or any matter, cause or thing whatsoever, prior to the
date hereof.

IN WITNESS WHEREOF, I have hereunto set my hand and seal this _____

Day of _____, 19 ____ .

WITNESS:

_____ (signature) _____
                                        (Claimant's signature)

INSTRUCTIONS:
        Read carefully, and please sign, have witnessed and return to:

                        Service Department
                        Manhattan Storage Co.
                        1411 Third Avenue
                        New York, N. Y. 10028

130

I called the company and reached an appropriate executive. After a certain amount of haggling during which I threw out several well-chosen legal-sounding terms ("allegations," "stipulations," *res ipsa loquitur*," and "commence an action" always come in handy), we reached an agreement. It was clear that neither of us considered this an important matter and that we both knew the company had a liability. I did point out that the originally proposed settlement of $95.50 was, in effect, returning less than the *premium* they had been paid for insuring our goods and that this was slightly outrageous in view of the actual damages. We agreed on a sum of two hundred fifty dollars according to the scheme below:

	Originally Claimed	Originally Allowed	Final Agreement
Horses	30	—	15
Color TV set	67.27	5	27.50
Piano	75	32.50	65
Dresser	50	15	15
Fish tank	10	10	10
Electric Typewriter	17.65	—	17.50
Tape Recorder	Repair or Replacement	—	30
Garrard Turntable	Repair or Replacement	—	37
Cupboard Turntable	10	10	10
Small Heritage Table	35	15	15
Medicine Bottles	5-10	8	8
	302.42 plus tape recorder and Garrard turntable	95.50	250

<u>RELEASE</u>

KNOW ALL MEN BY THESE PRESENTS

That (we)
~~XXX~~
(1)   MR. RALPH CHARELL

for and in consideration of REPAIRS   Dollars $ _____

" " "   "   " REPLACEMENT   Dollars $ _____

" " "   "   " CASH   Dollars $ __250.00__

" " "   "   "   Dollars $ _____

TOTAL SETTLEMENT $ __250.00__

subject to payment, to release and discharge and by these presents do for,
myself, my heirs, executors, administrators and assigns, release and for-
ever discharge   MORGAN AND BROTHER MANHATTAN STORAGE COMPANY, INC.
       and   ATLANTIC MUTUAL INSURANCE COMPANY

from any and all claims or demands by reason of my recent removal on or

about the   __17th__   day of __DECEMBER__   , 19 __71__

from __New York, New York__   to   __New York, New York__ ,
which I, my heirs, executors, administrators, or assigns can, shall or
may have any reason or any matter, cause or thing whatsoever, prior to the
date hereof.

IN WITNESS WHEREOF, I have hereunto set my hand and seal this _____

Day of _____, 19 ____.

WITNESS:

_____ (signature) _____
                                      (Claimant's signature)

<u>INSTRUCTIONS:</u>
      Read carefully, and please sign, have witnessed and return to:

              Service Department
              Manhattan Storage Co.
              1411 Third Avenue
              New York, N. Y. 10028

When I did not receive a check more than a week after returning the release I again called the company. I was informed that my landlord had not yet paid his share of the moving bill and that the claim would be settled only after he did. I replied that one of the conditions on which I had agreed to accept two hundred fifty dollars was that the receipt of that sum would not be delayed. In addition, I said, I had paid my share of the moving bill, and whether or not my landlord ever paid his share was no real concern of mine. I also pointed out that my former landlord was a man of great wealth and excellent reputation and would no doubt pay the bill very soon. But the representative of Morgan and Brother Manhattan Storage Company, Inc. was adamant.

As the proposed settlement was so close to the actual damages and the claim so small that I really did not want to spend much more time on it, I decided to try one more approach. I noticed that in the release form we were being asked to discharge from further liability not only the moving company but their insurance company, The Atlantic Mutual Insurance Company. I called the insurance company and explained the situation. I tried to make it clear that I was willing to limit their liability in this way but only if I received a check before the close of business that day. I pointed out that I usually bill between a hundred and a hundred fifty dollars an hour for my time and that at this point there was no way I could break even on this transaction. If I had to spend any further time on this matter, then all bets were off. I said this in a friendly and courteous but firm manner.

The insurance man called the moving company, and a messenger arrived later that day with the check and new release forms.

The Mail-Order Book

I received a four-page printed circular in the mail. It offered a book which was described as having been turned down by over thirty publishers as "too hot to handle." With two colors of ink and much underlining of words, exclamation points, and big letters, the circular promised that the book would tell the reader how to get almost everything he wanted *FREE*!

Although the book sounded a lot like Abbie Hoffman's *Steal this Book,* the title of the book described in the circular was not the same and the author's name was never mentioned. On the bare chance that there might be some overlap between the book offered and this book, which I was then writing, I enclosed my check in the amount of six dollars and ninety-eight cents and ordered the book.

I was rewarded with a standard-sized paperback book. The cover called it a "privately printed special edition" and was marked with a price of seven ninety-five. Although the title of the book was not *Steal This Book*, its author was Abbie Hoffman and the copyright page indicated that the book's former title was indeed *Steal This Book*.

Although I am a firm believer in freedom of the press, this book seemed to be carrying things rather far. At the back of the book there was even a mail-in coupon for ordering additional copies of the book under its original title at $1.95 per copy. Despite the fact that only about seven dollars was involved, I really couldn't ignore the incredible height of chutzpah to which I had been subjected. Unfortunately, I had thrown out the circular and the envelope in which it had come and all I had was the packaging which had contained the book. I wrote the following letter:

February 6, 1973

Gentlemen:

I was shocked to receive (title of book), for which I paid $6.98. Contrary to your promotional material which I received in the mail, this self-styled "privately printed special edition" is simply an edition of a completely different title that had been formerly published at a small fraction of this price by an author whom you conveniently failed to mention in the material I received.

Clearly, this paperback edition, which was

purchased by me in good faith, is something of a hoax and was purchased solely on the basis of misrepresentations and omissions. I will not make any further allegations at this time except to say that if I do not hear from you by return mail to the effect that my purchase price of $6.98 will be immediately forthcoming upon the return of this book, I intend to send the book and a copy of this correspondence and your promotional material which I received in the mail to my postmaster with instructions to investigate the possibilities of mail fraud.

Sincerely,
Ralph Charell

A couple of weeks later, having received no response, I called the post office in which the mail-order company's box was located. Unfortunately, nobody at the post office was able to give me the name or the address of any principal of the company. I told the post office that I was not alleging any impropriety but that it was my understanding that, under the postal regulations, anybody who bought material through the mail had an absolute right to know with whom he was dealing—that is, to get the name and address (other than simply the post office box) of an executive or an officer of the company.

The post office spokesman acknowledged that this was correct, but admitted, somewhat apologetically, that he did not have the information. However, he told me, if I requested it in writing, the post office would get it.

While I was waiting for a response to my letter I received another identical offer in the mail. I noticed that there was a money-back guarantee on the book, and that the envelope in which the circular had arrived had a Pitney Bowes meter number. I called the post office from which the envelope was mailed and requested the name and address of the company that had mailed it. This time I was able to get the information.

When I called this company, I was told that it was merely a mailing house; they had nothing to do with the company which had sold me the book except to do their mailing. I asked an executive of this company to put me in touch with the other company, but he said that would be impossible. He did agree to get in touch with the other company and would ask somebody in charge there to call me. I requested that the return call be made to me the same day. There was no response.

After a reasonable interval, I wrote to the post office to which I had originally sent my check and requested in writing the information which I had failed to get verbally.

When a response did not come within a reasonable time I called the postmaster to whom I had written. He informed me that his staff was still working on the matter, but that in an attempt to help me get my money back he would speak with the person who picked up the mail for the company.

He then wrote to me, asking me to have patience for a few more days and assuring me that my money would be returned. He asked me to return the book to him after I was reimbursed and said he would get it back to the company. I told him that as I usually bill between a hundred and a hundred and fifty dollars per hour for my time and that, as there was no way I could break even on this transaction, I would appreciate his asking the company to allow me to keep both the book and the money. He arranged that, and the check for the return of my money closed out the incident.

Underwear

On my way to an indoor pool, I picked up a set of underwear at Saks Fifth Avenue. Although I did not have my charge card with me, I showed the salesperson sufficient identification and signed for the eight dollar and three cent purchase. About a month later I received a bill for this amount and a notice advising me that although I did not have a charge account at Saks, the store would be happy to open one for me if I filled out the enclosed form.

What surprised me most was that the notice set forth both my name and address correctly. That being the case, I was somewhat at a loss as to why the store had failed to locate my account when I had been doing business with Saks for more than twenty years. I returned all of the material received with a handwritten note to this effect and asked them to kindly bill my account.

The following month I received another bill and

another notice telling me that I could open an account with the store by filling out the enclosed forms, but would I kindly remit payment in the meantime. Again, I returned all of the material with a handwritten note explaining the situation, across the top of which I wrote in large capitals: "FINAL NOTICE!" If they had sent a computer card I would have punched out some or all of the holes and thus gotten individual treatment.

When I received the same notice a month later, I called the store. The store manager was unavailable, but I was able to speak with one of his assistants.

I told this man that the store had had three opportunities to properly bill my account for the underwear and that if they had done so any one of these times this telephone call and one or both of the handwritten notes would not have been necessary. I explained that as I usually bill between a hundred and a hundred and fifty dollars an hour for my time, it seemed clear that there was no way I could break even on this transaction and that I had dealt with the store for a generation without too much difficulty. The man agreed with me and promised that I would not hear of the matter again.

Rakes and Fishes

My wife once arranged to meet our daughter after school at W & J Sloane, a large furniture store. As our daughter entered the store, a guard accosted her and ordered her out of the store. Leslie, a charming fifteen-year-old, asked the guard why. He refused to explain and merely repeated the order. She told the guard she had an appointment with her mother, who was waiting for her right there on the ground floor of the store. The guard, who didn't speak English fluently and perhaps did not understand her, again ordered her to leave.

Leslie suggested that a woman employee of the store who was standing nearby might accompany her to the rear of the first floor where her mother was waiting. The guard permitted this and followed a couple of steps behind as Leslie and the woman walked through the store. Unfortunately, at the precise moment they arrived at the appointed meeting place, my wife was bending down to inspect an antique and was not visible. This reactivated the guard, but just as he was preparing to descend on Leslie, she called out plaintively for her mother, who immediately stood up. When my wife learned what had happened, she was upset.

Leslie preferred to forget the matter, but my wife told her that the next child who came into the store might not be as resilient as she was. Julianne went up to the guard and asked him why he had ordered Leslie out of the store, but he ignored the question and walked away. When my wife asked his name he turned around and said, "I don't have to tell you that." At that point my wife discussed the matter with another person in security at the store, and, somewhat mollified, she and Leslie began to look for antiques.

Leslie picked out a small chest, on which two old, rusty pieces of metal had been placed. When my wife asked whether the two pieces of metal were included with the chest, the salesperson replied that she wasn't sure but would check. She came back to report that they were included. My wife purchased the chest and asked the salesperson to write up the purchase as including the two pieces of metal, which she did, calling the two pieces of metal "rakes."

The following day my wife received a call at home from somebody at Sloane's. He explained that the two pieces of metal did not actually come with the chest; they were an additional twenty-five dollars each and had been marked with price tags to that effect.

My wife told him that there had been no price tag on either of the two pieces of metal, and that the salesperson had assured her that they came with the chest. The caller said that, under the circumstances, they would honor the trade as originally agreed.

The next morning, a Saturday, we were awakened at about 9:15 by the woman who had sold my wife and daughter the chest and "rakes." The woman explained that she had made a mistake; the "rakes" were not included with the chest. I told her that my wife had discussed this with someone else at Sloane's who had decided to include them. I also told her that if there were any further problem she could call us again (but at a somewhat later hour) and we would work it out.

The following Wednesday my wife received a call from the same woman and was told that the entire order had been canceled. Julianne inquired who had canceled the order and on what authority, pointing out that the items she had bought were one of a kind and that nobody had the right to cancel the purchase. The woman replied that it had been done on a vice president's authority but that she could not divulge his name.

The following morning I phoned the president of the store. As he was not in, I spoke with his executive assistant. I explained the situation, including the *contretemps* with the guard, and stated that unless we received delivery of the chest and the two pieces of metal by the close of business, Sloane's was courting litigation. During the conversation I learned that the vice president who had canceled the order was a Mr. Chartreuse, that the chest was in a warehouse, and the two pieces of metal were at the store. I also learned that Sloane's was now calling the two pieces of metal "fishes" or "ealings" and since they were no longer "rakes" we had no claim to them.

I told the president's assistant that I did not intend to respond to that statement at that time, but that if all of the items purchased, by whatever name, were not delivered by the close of business, the store would have an opportunity to make that distinction to the judge.

I then called the warehouse in an attempt to arrange the immediate delivery of the chest, but my attempt failed. During lunch, I called the president's office again, was told that the president was not in, and asked his assistant whether the appropriate delivery orders had been given. I was told that nothing could be done unless Mr. Chartreuse rescinded the cancellation. However, Mr. Chartreuse had been in a closed session with union negotiators all day and probably would remain there through the night.

I told the assistant that it seemed a bit out of scale to withhold our purchase from us. My daughter was leaving town for the Easter vacation, and we wanted to have these items delivered before she left. Surely we could straighten out the matter in a satisfactory manner after we took delivery. Besides, I told him, there was some danger that the pieces would be lost or sold and they were one of a kind. I also pointed out that I usually bill between a hundred and a hundred and fifty dollars an hour for my time and that there was no way I could break even on this transaction. When it became apparent that my efforts were of no avail, I asked the assistant whether Sloane's was part of a larger company, and was told that City Stores was the parent company.

After lunch, I called City Stores and asked for the president. When I learned that he was not in, I explained that the call involved two pieces of litigation, and I was connected with the General Counsel. I told this man that he was speaking with an angry attorney and father and asked him to listen to the facts as I presented them as if he were in my position.

An intelligent, charming man, he agreed with me completely that the situation was outrageous and promised to call Mr. Chartreuse and have him make delivery of the chest and two pieces of metal. The man returned my call a few moments later and told me that he had spoken with Mr. Chartreuse. They had located the two pieces of metal in Mr. Chartreuse's private office many stories above the store and could certainly deliver them by the close of business, but were not sure they could get the chest to us by that time. This man said that he was going into a lengthy meeting but would turn the matter over to a Mr. Scarlet, an attorney, who would be getting back to me soon. He also told me that he had to call Mr. Chartreuse out of his meeting a second time, and that

Mr. Chartreuse had been incensed at being interrupted again to talk about rakes and fishes. I told him I was delighted to hear that and thanked him very much.

In a couple of subsequent conversations with Mr. Scarlet, I learned that the chest was being sent back to the store to be placed in a private cab with the pieces of metal and delivered as one package. I called my wife and told her to expect delivery in about an hour.

When I arrived home that evening, the chest and the two pieces of metal, also known as "rakes" or "fishes" or "ealings," had arrived by cab, gift-wrapped, and we had been billed the originally agreed price. The "rakes" or "fishes" or "ealings" looked to be worth about twenty-five cents apiece in a garage sale, but we are, of course, happy with them.

The following day, I called the store and told the woman who sold my wife the merchandise to call me if any problem developed.

PREVIOUS BALANCE	FINANCE CHARGE	PAYMENTS	CREDITS	CHARGES	NEW BALANCE AND BILLING DATE	MINIMUM PAYMENT DUE
				42.80	42.80 MAY 5	10.00

PAYMENTS OR CREDITS RECEIVED AFTER BILLING
DATE WILL APPEAR ON NEXT STATEMENT.

Your **FINANCE CHARGE** is based on a monthly periodic rate of **1½%** on balances up to
$500 and **1%** on any excess over **$500** which correspond to **ANNUAL PERCENTAGE
RATES** of **18%** and **12%** respectively. **FINANCE CHARGE** will be avoided if full payment
of the New Balance is received within **30** days of the billing date shown on each statement.
NOTICE: See reverse side and accompanying statement(s) for important information.

W & J Sloane

CREDIT APPROVAL	W&J Sloane, INC.	DEPT. NO. 50	C.O.D.	DRIVER COLLECT

SALESPERSON NAME GIBBERTI

DATE 3/9/73 CHG

321025

DELIVERY DATE 3/29 MON

SHIP NAME RALPH CHARELL

DATE SHIPPED
STREET

SHIPPED VIA
CITY New York STATE NY ZIP CODE SPECIAL

BUS. PHONE TEL. AREA CODE & NO. DEL. INSTR. ROUTE NO.

WITH OTHER GOODS ON SLSCK. NO. LOC./DEPT.

CHARGE NAME RALPH CHARELL
STREET
CITY New York STATE NY ZIP CODE

Special Instructions	FL.	SALESMAN 8706	DEPT. 50	RETAIL 40 00

FLR.
SAMPLE

FACT. NO.	PIECE NO.	QUAN	DESCRIPTION	EXTENSION
817	400	(1)	SMALL CHEST WITH RAKES	40 00

Rewritten from
S/C 768370

	SUB TOTAL	40 00
	SHIPPING SERVICE CHARGES	
	SALES TAX	2 80
	TOTAL	42 80

USE THIS BOX FOR COD ONLY
TOTAL AMOUNT $
LESS COD PAYMENT $
COD BALANCE DUE $

TAX CODE 0

This merchandise is being ordered to meet my specifications and is not subject to
cancellation or return for any reason for which W & J SLOANE is not responsible. If
cancelled or returned, this purchase is subject to a 25% forfeiture.

PURCHASER'S SIGNATURE

The Late Movie

One night my wife and I went to a neighborhood movie. We called the theatre to get the exact starting time and arrived at 9:55 PM, five minutes early. I paid the cashier seven dollars and we went in.

The lights were on as we entered the theatre. About twenty per cent of the seats were occupied and recorded music filled the air. As it was approximately 10 PM there was an air of expectancy which intensified each time a nondescript musical selection ended, but no film rolled. One by one, the minutes ticked slowly by. People began to look at the projectionist's booth; the crowd was becoming noticeably impatient.

There were two women seated behind my wife and me who looked as if they might be in their early thirties. At about 10:30, they began to complain about the delay.

"Wouldn't it be something," I said to my wife, "if

the entire audience suddenly left and demanded their money back."

"What a great idea!" said one of the women behind us. "Let's do it!"

"What do you think?" I asked my wife. "This picture is playing over on the West Side. We could probably get there in about ten minutes by cab."

"I don't care much one way or the other. It's up to you," she said.

"Let's go."

Julianne and I walked up the aisle. The two women seated behind followed us. Everybody else in the theatre remained seated.

I walked up to the cashier and presented our ticket stubs.

"It's now 10:35," I said. "The picture hasn't begun. We'd like to have our money back."

The cashier explained that returning our money would have to be approved by the assistant manager. While we waited for him to appear, I asked why his approval was necessary. Because it was, I was informed.

At length, the assistant manager came out and demanded to know our names and addresses before our money could be returned. I told him that I preferred not to give him our names and addresses but that we had been delayed almost three-quarters of an hour and that I usually bill between a hundred and a hundred and fifty dollars an hour for my time. Unfortunately, I was wearing an old sweater and sneakers with torn and knotted shoelaces and thus probably looked, to the uniformed assistant manager, like a person whose time was worth considerably less. He told me rather peremptorily that unless I supplied the information he requested I could not expect to get the money back. I asked to see the manager of the theatre. The two women also refused to give their names and addresses.

The theatre manager arrived some minutes later.

"Ya want ya money back, ya gotta sign ya name and address."

"I prefer not to do so."

"Ya don't sign, ya don't get ya money back."

"I prefer not to give hostile people my name and address and I don't see any reason to do so."

"That's O.K. with me."

"Look, don't be unpleasant. I could sign a fictitious name. What would that prove?"

"Ya want ya money back, ya gotta sign ya name and address."

"Fine," said I. "Just give me a receipt indicating that I paid the seven dollars and that we left without seeing any part of the film. I'm sure I can be reimbursed later by the theatre chain."

"I ain't givin' ya no receipts."

"In that case, since you are holding our money unjustly and refuse to return it, I will be obliged to call a cop."

"You do that," said the theatre manager and he left.

The situation had deteriorated quickly and I was beginning to feel somewhat foolish. The two women thought it was a terrific idea to call a cop.

I looked at my wife somewhat sheepishly, shrugged, and left to call the local precinct. Several minutes later, a patrol car arrived. I explained the situation and asked one of the policemen to accompany me to the manager's office so that he could be properly identified.

The manager was somewhat surprised to see the policeman and me in his office.

"As you have refused to return our money, I am afraid I must ask you to identify yourself."

The manager reached into a desk drawer, withdrew a business card and handed it to the policeman, who handed it to me.

"This card appears to have his business address," I told the policeman. "I would like to have his home address."

"I don't have to give him no home address," insisted the theatre manager.

"Hm," said I. "You insisted on getting *my* home address before you would return our money. Now, you won't give me *your* home address when I want to identify you so I can sue for the return of my money. It doesn't seem right."

"Why don't you give him your home address?" the police officer asked.

At that moment, the other policeman joined us in the manager's office and quickly took charge.

"He doesn't have to supply his home address."

As my wife and I left the theatre, the two women were giving their names and addresses to the assistant manager. A few minutes later, we were whisked to a theatre on the West Side and saw the same film, although not from the beginning. At 1:30 AM, after we had waited to see the opening of the film and were hailing a cab, the West Side theatre district seemed considerably less safe than our neighborhood. On the way home, I apologized to my wife for the inconvenience and conceded that I had not handled the situation too brilliantly.

The next day, I called the division manager of the theatre chain and related the facts.

Two days later I received a letter from that gentleman:

"Dear Sir:

Enclosed find check for twelve dollars ($12.00) to cover out of pocket expense incurred in your recent unpleasant visit to our   theatre on   , New York City.

I have taken action which I feel will eliminate the possibility of similar treatment being given to any future patron.

Thank you for bringing this to our attention. The incident will be used in a managers' meeting as a horrible example of public relations.

Very truly yours,"

Still Number One

Mr. Sky Blue
Hertz
660 Madison Avenue
New York, New York 10021

Dear Mr. Blue:

About a week in advance, I reserved a car to be
picked up at the 76th Street near First Avenue Hertz
at 10:00 AM on July 7 and returned to the same location
the early evening of the same day. Ms. C. Coffee confirmed that reservation. On July 6, I reconfirmed the
reservation so as to be absolutely sure a car would
be available.

When I went to pick up the car I was told there
would be a four-hour wait. "I assume you heard what
I just said," was the discourteous way this information

was imparted. My shock and indignation were probably apparent. Why hadn't anybody called me in advance so as to give me an opportunity to make other plans? They were too busy. Why couldn't two people do this while the third made the few calls? No response.

As my wife was about to leave our apartment to meet me downstairs, I asked for a telephone so that she would not have to stand in the street wondering what had happened to me while I tried to work out some new arrangement. Instead of offering me the use of one of the idle telephones, I was directed across the garage to a public telephone and, unfortunately, just missed my wife.

I noticed that people who had Hertz #1 reservations were getting cars. I asked to speak with the person in charge at that location and explained that I had reserved the car a week in advance, reconfirmed the previous day, and as the term of the rental was only half a day, every hour of further delay was important. I asked whether there were any other cars in the garage. Not only were there no cars, but they had even sent out all of their cars without spare tires. I asked whether there was a car at La Guardia and was told there was none. When I inquired how this was possible and suggested it be checked by telephone, it was so checked and I was told a car was being held for me at La Guardia. I asked for the license number of that car and was informed that it wasn't actually being held, but would be there shortly. When I responded that my wife and I would be at La Guardia by taxi within half an hour and didn't want any further delay and demanded the license number of a car that would be there, the person in charge asked for the *make* of the car and told me it was a Plymouth Fury. When I insisted on the license number, that required another call and further delay. The license number was given as 212ZDV.

Drenched with perspiration, I then went to pick up my wife, who had been standing in the street for more than half an hour. Nobody at Hertz offered to reimburse us for the taxi fare, which I should have thought was a routine courtesy.

We had planned to have an early lunch with friends near Poughkeepsie, visit and swim with other friends near Brewster, and leave Brewster about 7:00 PM in order to avoid night driving on a weekend notorious for automobile accidents. As we had planned to eat lunch early, we had had virtually nothing for breakfast.

Because of the delays involved, we decided to cancel our first stop, but our friends' line was busy and we were pressed for time, so we took a cab to La Guardia. By the time we called from La Guardia our lunch, which we were canceling, was being elaborately prepared. We were therefore compromised into promising to stop off to see our friends in Poughkeepsie on the way home from Brewster.

Without going into all of the unpleasant details, this occasioned our driving almost 150 miles, mostly on unlighted roads in the middle of the night, with a right directional signal that was out of order (as subsequently reported to Hertz) and feeling weak with hunger as our plans for meals had been destroyed.

When we arrived at Hertz at 2:00 AM to return the

car, my hip and back in spasm, we found the place closed for the night, a fact nobody had called to our attention earlier. This necessitated my hobbling out of bed Sunday morning to return the car.

On top of the costs to me in terms of time, nervous tension, and strain to my wife and me, hunger, ruined plans for us and our friends and their children, taxi fares and long-distance telephone calls, safety, loss of sleep and a second trip to return the car, I am being billed $49.21 for the use of the car for half a day (as per enclosed copy of bill). This seems analogous to billing the poison victim for the cost of the poison.

I think I am a pretty loyal and good customer and I would like an ameliorating and timely response to this series of failures. Please do not turn this letter over to somebody who has, by virtue of the repetitiousness of handling complaints, begun to think of the customer as the enemy.

If #1 fails to maintain its standards, it soon becomes Brand X.

Sincerely,
Ralph Charell

P.S. The promised Plymouth Fury, license number 212ZDV, was unavailable because of further mishandling but we were able to get a Ford.

7128728 9

SHOW THIS NO. ON ALL CORRESPONDENCE

THIS IS YOUR ORIGINAL INVOICE
PLEASE REMIT PAYMENT IN THE
ENVELOPE PROVIDED.

Hertz

To:

0010 353   3 NA

NEW YORK NY

BASIC CHARGE ONE DAY PLUS MILEAGE

CAR CHECKED IN AT AREA/LOC/CITY/STATE

TIME IN	7/8/73	9 NA
TIME OUT		

RATES — FOR RENTALS WITH ONE DAY ONLY:

INCLUDE ☒   DO NOT INCLUDE ☐

	MINIMUM RENTAL	EXTRA DAYS	EXTRA HOURS	MILEAGE ALLOWED (If Any)	EXTRA MILES
GASOLINE		DAYS			

MILEAGE IN	21978	DAYS	18
MILEAGE OUT	21777	HRS 3-	
MILES DRIVEN	201	WKS 90	
MILEAGE ALLOWED (If Any)			
MILES CHARGED		MILES @ 18	36 18

CAR RENTED AT (CITY/STATE)	AREA & LOCATION NO.
LA GUARDIA AIRPORT	1901

CAR TO BE CHECKED IN AT CITY/STATE   LOC. NO.   DATE DUE

CREDIT CARD	NO. 1 CLUB NO. CREDIT APPROVAL
OTHER IDENTIFICATION	C.D.P. I.D. NO.
DRIVER'S LICENSE NO. STATE EXPIRES	

VEHICLE NO.

CAR LIC. NO.	STATE
CAR MAKE	BODY STYLE
OWNING CITY/STATE	Nyc.

SUBTOTAL	418
	280 108
SUBTOTAL	43 3
SERVICE CHARGE	

HOME OR BUSINESS ADDRESS

CITY/STATE   New York NY   ZIP CODE

I HAVE READ THE TERMS & CONDITIONS ON PAGE 1 (OTHER SIDE) AND PAGE 2 OF THIS RENTAL AGREEMENT AND AGREE THERETO.
I AUTHORIZE HERTZ TO PROCESS A CREDIT CARD VOUCHER, IF ANY, IN MY NAME FOR CHARGES HEREUNDER.

X

Thank You For Renting From Hertz

GASOLINE QUANTITY

IN	F	¾	½	¼	E
OUT	F	¾	½	¼	E

REFUELING SERVICE

ACCEPTS COLLISION DAMAGE WAIVER (CDW)   DECLINES CDW:
CDW X   X

CDW (Per Day) 2.00	2
SUBTOTAL	45 3

ACCEPTS PERSONAL ACCIDENT INSURANCE (PAI)   DECLINES PAI:
PAI X   X

TAX 6.3%	2 86
PAI (Per Day) 1.00	

— RESERVATION DATA —

RESERVATION I.D. NO.   COMMISSION NO.   PREPAID   YES ☐ NO ☐

REMARKS:

CASH REFUND

EXPLANATION   AMOUNT

I ACKNOWLEDGE RECEIPT OF ABOVE AMOUNT:
X

DEPOSIT   none

TOTAL CHARGES	49 21
LESS GAS-OIL-REPAIRS	
NET DUE	49 21
LESS DEPOSIT (If Any)	

R/A PREPAID BY (LAST NAME)

R/A COMPLETED BY (LAST NAME)

NET DUE 49 21

DRB DATE   PAID BY (X)   CASH   CHECK   CENT BILL   INTL BILL   GUAR ANTEED REG.   LOCAL REG.

Original Invoice No. **7128728 9**

405 (11/72)

LA GUARDIA AIRPORT, N.Y. 1901

Hertz

THIS IS YOUR ORIGINAL INVOICE

PAYMENT DUE UPON RECEIPT. PLEASE DETACH THIS STUB AND RETURN WITH YOUR PAYMENT TO:

THE HERTZ CORPORATION
P.O. BOX 26141
OKLAHOMA CITY, OKLAHOMA 73126

Mr. Blue responded with "most sincere apologies" and an explanation as to why Hertz occasionally cannot meet reservations on schedule. He also canceled the $49.21 charge as "adding insult to injury." He then extended additional apologies to my wife and me and enclosed an application for a Hertz Number One Club which he promised to process personally.

Hertz is still Number One with me thanks to sensitive, intelligent executives like Mr. Sky Blue. I responded immediately and await my membership in the Hertz Number One Club.

Con Ed

Before my wife and I were married, I lived in many different sections of Manhattan. It seemed to me that each time I left an apartment, my final Con Edison bill was unusually high. I was aware that usage of gas and electricity can vary from month to month, and the apparent overcharges were small, so I never bothered to check them.

After we were married, we both received our final Con Edison bills in our new apartment at about the same time. We both felt certain we were being overcharged, although by only a few dollars.

I called the company and reported that I thought I had been overcharged on my final bill. Although I was assured that my complaint would be looked into and I would be hearing from them, I never did. I called and spoke with a succession of people who assured me that they would look into this matter but nobody ever got back to me. I had a list of the names of the people with whom I had spoken and the dates and times, and the list kept growing.

Finally I told the bottom name on the list that this would be my last call. If the matter were not quickly checked and a response made within a reasonably short period of time, I intended to place the matter in the hands of the Public Service Commission. That call, too, was never returned.

As promised, I called the PSC and outlined the situation. The PSC man told me that Con Edison was still using the archaic method of sending men to individual premises to read meters. If the reader failed to gain access to the premises for any reason, the company had the right to estimate the bill. In the case of final bills, there was a tendency to estimate the bills on the high side.

In that case, I suggested, the new tenant in my old apartment would be getting the benefit of this high estimate, and I would likewise get a bonus from the former tenant in my new apartment. Although strictly speaking not entirely correct, it might be acceptable for a tenant to overpay a final bill and underpay an initial bill in the new premises, but my initial bills had never been low, to the best of my recollection.

The PSC man explained that any use of gas or electricity by the building superintendent, painters, or other workmen in making the apartment ready for the new tenant would tend to close that gap. In fact, if an apartment is left vacant for some length of time and the utilities are used fairly regularly during that interim, it is possible for both the new and the old tenant to be overcharged. In fact, the PSC man explained, if the company estimated the final bill on the high side and then took readings, these lower readings might be used as a starting point for billing the new tenant. Although a certain amount of usage by painters, workmen, etc. would not be that of the new tenant, he or she would be billed for all such usage.

I concluded that an old tenant whose bill had been estimated on the high side should receive a rebate, and said that I had never received such a rebate. The PSC man advised me that if I requested it, the Public Service Commission could require Con Ed to furnish individual printouts for gas and electricity, which would make any overcharge readily apparent.

I made the request and soon received two large worksheets which did in fact indicate overcharges. The amounts were immediately credited to my account at Con Edison.

I'd Rather Do it Myself

A few years ago I hired a lawyer to help me adopt my (then) stepdaughter and asked him to proceed as quickly as possible. He assured me that he would get to work on the matter immediately.

Every few weeks I called him to inquire how soon the actual adoption would take place. Each time he explained that he had been extremely busy but would be getting to it at once.

About a year after I'd engaged his services, I called the lawyer and told him that unless the procedure could be commenced during that week, I would simply hire someone else. He informed me matter-of-factly that he had become increasingly involved in various business pursuits and had actually given up the practice of law. He regretted all of the delays in commencing the adoption proceeding but, with my permission, he would call another attorney immediately and get back to me that very day. In addition, he would inform the other attorney of the need for speed.

Later that day, the other attorney called and told me that he would be happy to undertake the adoption for me at once. How much might that cost? Well, his usual fee for such a matter was five hundred dollars, but as the first attorney was waiving his remittance fee, he would be able to accept only three hundred. He promised to get to work on it at once.

During that week, I went to Boston on a business trip. As I had some work to do *en route*, I decided to take the train. About an hour out of Boston, a man sat down next to me and struck up a conversation. He was an attorney, a graduate of Yale Law School, and had been practicing for about thirty years. I asked him what a reasonable attorney's fee should be for a routine adoption. I explained that the child was living with her natural mother and stepfather and that the natural father had agreed to give his written consent to the adoption. The child, of course, had also agreed.

He replied that such a matter was indeed routine and involved the filling out of four pieces of paper and appearing briefly before a judge. His fee would ordinarily be one hundred twenty-five dollars for handling such a matter but, he volunteered offhandedly, he would do it for me for only one hundred dollars.

I told him that I had spoken with a lawyer recently who told me that his standard fee in such a case was five hundred dollars. My companion made it clear that unless tycoons or wealthy celebrities were involved, five hundred dollars was exorbitant. I agreed that it seemed excessive for half a morning's work and asked the man if he would handle such a matter for me. He agreed, and we exchanged business cards.

The following day, I called the attorney who had been referred to me. I told him that I wished to disengage his services and asked what he had done on the matter to date and how much I owed him. He told me that as he had done nothing, I owed him nothing. I thanked him and asked the lawyer I had met on the train to proceed immediately, which he promised to do.

A couple of days later, I received the four pieces of paper which he had mentioned. The covering letter requested the immediate payment of one hundred twenty-five dollars in advance. I had the forms filled out and responded by telling him that I had no objection to the price of one hundred twenty-five dollars (despite the fact that he had volunteered to handle the matter for one hundred dollars) but I did not usually pay in full for services before they were rendered. I enclosed a check in the amount of forty dollars on account and asked him whether it was acceptable. With that, I sent off all the forms, properly executed and duly notarized.

When I had heard nothing from the man for about two weeks, I called his office and asked him when we could go before the judge. The man seemed surprised by my question and said that we could do that as soon as I got the papers to him. With a sinking feeling, I told him that I had done so about two weeks earlier. The man said that he had never received them. I was, of course, elated with the news that the entire set of original papers had been lost.

"In that case, I think I'm going to handle this matter myself, if you don't mind," said I. "Please let me know whether I owe you anything for your services at this point."

The man assured me that as he had done nothing I owed him nothing. I thanked him and suggested that, if he found my check for partial payment, he destroy it.

I immediately called the clerk of the Surrogate's Court and told him that I wished to have the four forms required to begin an adoption proceeding. The man asked me if I were a practicing attorney and I said no.

"Then I'm sorry," said the man, "but I cannot let you have those forms."

"Why not?"

"Because only an attorney may file for adoption."

"But that's outrageous," I said. "I'm a citizen and a taxpayer. Why don't I have the right to file the papers?"

"Because under the law a lawyer has to identify you before the judge."

"Why should a lawyer, who may never have seen me before we meet in court, have some mystical powers of identification? I'm sure that my wife and the child can identify me, and I can identify myself with all sorts of documents."

"The law requires a lawyer to identify you."

"Look, if we have to, we can take my fingerprints and submit those. This is my wife's child. We all live together right now. And we have the natural father's consent. I think it's outrageous that I have to hire a lawyer to do this. As a matter of fact, I have already hired three lawyers and they've done nothing but waste a lot of time. If you don't send me the forms I intend to go before a judge and demand them."

The man agreed to send the papers and told me to come and see him when they were properly executed. He would check them and, if they were in order, he would make an appointment with the judge for my wife, stepdaughter, and me. He informed me that when we went before the judge it would be necessary for us to be accompanied by a lawyer but that there would be such a person in the courtroom who would join us in the judge's chambers.

I had the papers filled out (again) and the matter went exactly as he had outlined. After the judge had signed the adoption papers and we left, I thanked the attorney who had identified me (I had met him about two minutes before we entered the judge's chambers) and asked him how much I owed him for his services. The man told me that there would be no charge at all but I insisted on handing him twenty-five dollars over his repeated objections. The entire proceeding, from the time I called the clerk of the court to the time we went out to lunch to celebrate, took approximately three weeks.

Keeping Cool

My wife bought an air conditioner at Macy's for our daughter's bedroom. It was scheduled to be installed the following Friday morning, and Julianne waited at home all day for it to arrive. After lunch, she began a series of telephone calls to the store. Because the company that installed the air conditioners was not part of Macy's, she was told, it was difficult to say precisely when the installers might show up. As night fell, it became obvious that the installation would not take place on the day agreed.

Julianne phoned the installation company and explained that we were going away the following day, but if the air conditioner could be installed early in the morning, all would be well. She was assured that we would be first on the list on Saturday.

Shortly before noon, a small platoon of bedraggled-looking young "installers" arrived with the air conditioner. Visions of this heavy piece of machinery hurtling from our window onto unsuspecting passersby danced through my mind. To the barely suppressed derision of the platoon, I oversaw the installation and made certain that nothing short of a few sticks of dynamite could loosen the air conditioner from its moorings.

On the next business day, I called Macy's and told a man in the Major Appliances department that my wife had wasted an entire day waiting in vain for the promised installation. In addition, our plans for the following day had been ruined by the tardiness, not to say lack of candor, shown by the installation company. Furthermore, my daughter had discovered that one of the controls on the air conditioner was not secured in the usual way with a set screw, but had been temporarily held in place with putty. I told the Macy's man that both the goods and the services involved here seemed less than first-rate, and that my best response would probably be to have the machine removed and the transaction rescinded.

The man was responsive. He said that he hoped I would be reasonable and offered to "absorb" the installation charges and to credit twenty-five dollars to our account against the purchase price. I found the arrangement acceptable.

Complain Now, Pay Later

In a volatile, ever-changing world, one of the few constants on which we may still rely is the incompetence of others. If preemptive complaining can preserve your nerve endings from untimely destruction at the hands of incompetents, it is clearly an important club to pack in your bag. By anticipating the incompetence of others and acting as if it has already been manifested, even the novice complainer can bypass the wearying early rounds of confrontation unscathed and come to the crucial endgame refreshed and in full control of an overpowering position.

Say you finally succumb to a local television commercial and mail in a check for the *Highlights of 2,000 Years of Western Thought and Philosophy in Prose, Poetry and Song* on three long-playing records plus, as a bonus for speed, the opening eleven notes of fifty beloved nondenominational hymns, the final two bars of thirty-seven ever-popular arias and the words and music of fifteen all-time favorite *Legal Holiday Tunes of the Free World,* all for only $5.95.

Whereupon, in the typical case, if you live in South Dakota, the merchandise will be shipped to South Carolina or not at all, and by the time you realize that it hasn't arrived and strain your resources of time, money and health trying to get delivery, you are no longer capable of enjoying the purchase, should it eventually arrive unbroken.

The "complain now, pay later" approach permits those who prefer results to recriminations to begin with the solution instead of the problem. Instead of sending in the check and then waiting uneasily for the occasion to complain, simply reverse the process. Complain first, and then send the check. The value of this simple strategem can only be fully appreciated by those whose carefully measured complaints have slowly given way, in the endless shuttling and shuffling of their calls for help, to incoherent whines or helpless whimperings, as time and countless retellings abraded their mettle to dust.

By complaining first, all of the outrage and most of the emotional investment are removed. In a calm, firm voice, you explain that it is not the money but the merchandise which is your primary concern. And then, in your best *noblesse oblige* manner, you insist on sending in "another" check, but this time addressed personally to the compassionate individual at the other end of the line.

When this is followed up with a check and a covering letter addressed to that individual, in which you first refer to the great understanding he showed in your pleasant conversation and then request his personal help in expediting shipment, particularly in view of "the original failure," well, you can practically hear the flourish of trumpets as the letter is read and almost see the speeded-up action which follows.

A Case of Forbearance

On our return from a recent vacation, my wife and I arrived at JFK Airport at about two o'clock in the morning and began to look for a taxi. The flight had been late, we were tired and hungry, and my back was in spasm. After a long wait, I was lucky enough to spot a vacant cab, and hailed it. The cab stopped, but its doors were locked.

"Where are you going?" asked the driver.

"Manhattan."

"Which side?"

"East."

"All right," said the driver, "but I've got to pick up a couple of people."

"How many people?"

"Two, but I'll drop you home first."

"All right," said I, wearily. "My wife and four pieces of luggage are over there."

The driver parked the cab near the curb. While my wife entered the cab, I put two bags into the trunk and went off to get the remaining two suitcases. By the time I returned to the cab, the driver was tying several pieces of luggage onto the trunk; the lid, which would not close, hung at an angle which completely blocked the rear window. I put the two bags into the back seat and got in.

The "two people" the driver had to pick up turned out to be a family of five. Two adults rode in the front seat with the driver, one child sat on a jump seat, and the other two children shared the back seat with us. Because the trunk door could not be closed, frigid January air flowed into the back seat. The children were coughing, my wife was freezing, and I was squeezed into a small corner of the seat as we sped toward Manhattan with our rear view obstructed.

We made our labyrinthine way toward the East River and somewhere in the Nineties the family of five and I alighted from the cab. They paid the driver the total amount on the meter plus the bridge toll, collected their baggage, and left.

"You know," said I, removing my two bags from the trunk, "this is outrageous. You told me there were going to be two people and there were five; you told me that you would take us home first and you're taking us home last."

The driver re-entered the cab without replying. I placed the remaining two suitcases inside and rejoined my wife. As we approached our building,

I asked the driver to go around the block so I would not have to carry the four bags across the street. He made an illegal U-turn and pulled up to our door. After my wife and I got the luggage out of the cab, I said to the driver:

"How much do I owe you for this extremely uncomfortable and unsafe ride?"

"Eleven dollars," he said, indicating the meter, which for some unaccountable reason was still running.

I don't know why I didn't just pay it and leave. Surely, it wasn't the money—I had just spent about fifteen hundred dollars for a week's vacation. But I guess I wasn't too happy with the way the driver had handled things in general.

"I'll give you eight."

"Oh, yeah!" said the driver. "Then I'm taking you into the precinct for theft of services."

I decided that chutzpah of this magnitude could not go unchallenged.

"That's fine," said I. "Let's go."

Whereupon, we and the luggage found ourselves inside the cab again and, with the meter still running, we drove off.

"Where's the precinct?" asked the driver.

"I have no idea."

We rode along for a while until the driver broke the silence:

"I'm taking you back to Kennedy Airport."

"Would you mind repeating that?" I asked.

"I'm taking you back to Kennedy Airport," he said unmistakably.

My wife and I looked at one another in silence.

"Mr. Violet," I said, reading his name from the card on the dash, "I am an attorney. You are in the process of kidnaping my wife and me and unless you turn this cab about now and take us home and gently place our baggage out on the sidewalk and leave quietly, I am going to have you arrested by the first policeman we see. You are going to spend the night in jail. I am going to sign a complaint on a charge of kidnaping and use my best efforts to see that you get the maximum penalty mandated by law."

... which he totally ignored, and we continued to speed toward Kennedy Airport at about three o'clock in the morning. Twice again I pointed out to the driver that he was engaged in a serious crime to which heavy penalties were attached—but he made no response, except perhaps to increase our speed a few more miles above the limit.

When we got to the Triboro Bridge toll, the driver slowed down in the exact change lane. My wife and I flung open the doors of the cab. She began to blow her taxi whistle, and I screamed out to the tollkeeper.

"Help! We're being kidnaped! Save us! Help!"

The toll keeper ran out of the toll booth and for an instant looked into the cab. Then he ran across the roadway and we hoped that, as in the television movies, we would soon see the flashing red light and hear the siren which would presage our rescue. But, when no such drama ensued, we realized that our hopes had been unfounded.

"He probably radioed ahead," I told my wife, but we both knew I was kidding. We had some difficulty closing the cab doors as our lunatic driver picked up speed and roared off.

It must have finally dawned upon the driver that perhaps there actually was some jeopardy attached to what he was doing, for at a point between LaGuardia and Kennedy airports, he stopped the cab on a shoulder and said:

"I'm dumping you out here."

I locked the cab doors so that I could discuss the attractiveness of that alternative with my wife. The driver activated a mechanism in the front of the cab, opened the lock, and tore the door open. He picked up our baggage and roughly placed it outside the cab. He then ordered us out. I complied and told my wife that if she would join me outside we would have the rest of our lives to consider our response.

By a lucky chance, a vacant cab approached and I rushed out to hail it. As it stopped, our former driver had a few more words to say:

"Don't stop," he instructed the other driver. "Don't pick them up. Keep going!"

"We're in deep trouble," said I. "We live in Manhattan. Please take us home. Just get us out of here."

"Get in," said the driver, which we did, as our

former driver raced off toward Kennedy Airport.

When we had gotten into the cab with our baggage, I asked the new driver to note the time, the way our baggage had been thrown onto the roadway, the fact that we were facing in exactly the opposite direction from where we wanted to go, and to remember that the other driver had instructed him not to pick us up because we had just been kidnaped and he might be called upon to testify as to what he had seen and heard.

The driver said that he would be happy to do so and we arrived home without further incident. As I had to be at the office in a few hours, my wife and I, after laughing all the way up in the elevator, probably out of relief, decided to get some sleep and compare notes in the morning.

It seemed to me that if I could show that the driver was acting in the course of his employment, I had an excellent case against the cab company. Because we were passengers and the driver was going to take us to the precinct for alleged theft of services and had the meter running for much of the ride after he announced that decision, I thought we had a strong case.

Before calling the Taxi and Limousine Commission I decided to check with a lawyer friend of mine. I had mentally conjured a settlement of several thousand dollars, tax-free.

The lawyer agreed that the way we had been treated at the airport was outrageous, but advised me to pass up this opportunity. He reminded me that when I had a matter involving a former landlord, I was dealing with responsible and reputable businessmen where all that was at stake was dollars. In this case, however, he pointed out that we would be going against an obviously unstable and unpredictable adversary, who, if we were successful, would undoubtedly be put out of his present business. Although the insurance company would pay the actual judgment, the driver would be cut off from his accustomed source of income and his reaction might expose my family and me to real danger. He strongly advised me not to go forward with the action.

My wife and I followed his advice and we've never regretted it.

Legal Advice

The fact that an individual of good will risks his property and his reputation—indeed, his personal freedom—by proffering free legal advice is by no means accidental. The laws which create such risks are drafted and adopted, in the main, by lawyers who prefer to be paid a fee by each individual to whom they dispense such advice. In a good cause, however, certain personal risks are often warranted. Therefore, a final practical word of legal advice.

There may occasionally arise a concatenation of circumstances so tangled, an adversary of such obduracy, or a wrong so grievous, as to seem to require the services of a firm of first-rate solicitors. If one does not already have such a firm on retainer, the chances of hiring one at a break-even cost, even assuming one's cause is victorious, are virtually nonexistent, for the number of top-flight law firms is small and their practice is more or less confined to large corporations and extremely wealthy individuals and some of their progeny.

In the past, those not among the wealthy or famous were forced to hire second-rate (or lesser) legal champions. These overburdened (and overpaid) officers of the court do a volume business, slowly grinding various matters through the machinery of the law. The more cases they have in their files, the greater their incomes, and the less time they have to devote to each case. Thus, there is a pressure in favor of letting the client's case lie in its file folder while built-in and other delays (often of the lawyer's own creation) wear down his client's will and expectations. Eventually, the case at hand will more than likely be compromised by the attorneys by telephone or in a brief meeting, leaving them free to slowly prosecute the next order of business and to bill their respective clients for at least some of the time that has been purposefully wasted.

Happily, there is an alternative. Because the overwhelming majority of cases never go to trial, and as second-rate (or lesser) counsel often hurt your case by creating a feeling of smug overconfidence in the greed centers of your adversaries when your attorney's failings are displayed, my advice is: instead of a lawyer, simply hire an actor to play the part of your lawyer in the typical case. At a small fraction of the usual cost, an actor of your selection will be happy to put in an appearance for you. And what an appearance! You may choose from a long list of talents that range from supercilious, pinstriped British types to shrill, overbearing dwarfs. One word of warning: it might be taken amiss if you refer to the actor as your attorney, but who may object if you say that Mr. So-and-So represents you or simply refer to him by name—"Mr. So-and-So will respond to that at an appropriate time and place." And, of course, the choice of his name is yours. He might be Calder Price-Jones II, Col. Aston Richardson or Col. Richard Astonson, Baba Au Rhum, etc.

Your surrogate lawyer may affect a physical handicap to advantage. Hearing aids, elaborate back and/or neck braces, canes and the like may be rented inexpensively. One useful opening might be to arrive about forty minutes late with one's representative advancing at a deliberate pace on a pair of canes—or, perhaps, wearing a hearing aid and deliberately failing to comprehend. These and similar approaches can easily hasten the journey of your adversary up the far wall.

Your representative may be an individual of great personal charm or overbearing pomposity, a bore or a spellbinder. Race and sex are also optional. Should you come upon a particularly effective actor, by all means recommend him to your friends. If not, pay him for the day's work and try again. In fact, it might be useful to fire him on the spot and settle your own case after he has slunk from the room.

Added to the advantages of nominal cost, desired appearance and personality, and impressive name, your actor/representative is your best choice in a number of other particulars. Clearly, you are in complete control since, lacking the power to compromise your rights, he cannot be corrupted by the other side. Nor, as is often the case with attorneys, can he pressure you, directly or indirectly, to accept the other side's ridiculous first offer. Additionally, you, the client, will not be intimidated by your representative as is the case in the typical lawyer/client relationship. You will also not find him difficult or impossible to speak with, because you have purchased his time on a preemptive basis.

As a matter of tactics, it cannot hurt to have him interrupt all statements by the other side over a short paragraph in length with: "Allegations. Merely allegations," or "I'm going to have to object to that," or "If we must, we will have to seek our remedy in an appropriate forum," delivered with a disarming smile.

As for how the other side responds to your representative, two obvious courses are an answering service or an arrangement with some out-of-town hotel, carefully booked in advance and just as carefully canceled long after the purpose has been served.

For those to whom a friend has not already recommended an effective actor/representative, a talent agent is only a telephone call away. And remember, when it comes to settlement, keep your expectations high.

Epilogue

In the taxi kidnaping example, my reason for forbearance was quite simply fear. However, lest the wrong impression be conveyed, I should add that I recommend and often practice forbearance out of purer motives. I have, for example, been in at least a half dozen minor taxicab accidents and have never considered instituting any action or claim in such cases.

Perhaps, if I were more saintly, the number of adversary situations in which I do get involved would be lower. However, as a practical matter, I realize that despite my efforts at forbearance, I will probably continue to slug it out on a selective basis whenever the circuits become overloaded.

If only there were a way of preventing such altercations—perhaps a badge or other means of warning malefactors that they are sure to come out second best if they decide to deal out their nonsense at me.

But there are no magic wands in big cities. Nonverbal communication can help, but it's imperfect.

If, however, one cannot sufficiently communicate one's prowess at countering chutzpah, one can be sensitive to the good and bad vibrations of others and, whenever practicable, seek out the former and avoid the latter long before they have escalated into an incident. People like Fred Astaire or Princess Grace and others of irresistible charm and celebrity are easily recognized and instantly accorded preferential treatment in most civilized jurisdictions. The rest of us, whether we fly down to Rio or stay closer to home, will probably have to continue to accept the hazards of the only game in town.

How one reacts to a given provocation, real or imagined, is always problematic. That judgment rests with the individual, and reasonable people may differ in their handling of a specific incident. Many counter poor treatment by simply choosing not to do any further business with such places. Others create Federal cases on the slightest pretext. All that is suggested here is that an attempt be made to maintain a sense of balance, a sense of propriety, and, above all, a sense of humor.